D1272042

Options on Foreign Exchange

Second Edition

Wiley Series in Financial Engineering

Options on Foreign Exchange

Second Edition

David F. DeRosa

John Wiley & Sons, Inc.

New York • Chichester • Weinheim • Brisbane • Singapore • Toronto

Library of Congress Cataloging-in-Publication Data:
DeRosa, David F.
    Options on foreign exchange / David F. DeRosa. — 2nd ed.
        p.   cm. — (Wiley series in financial engineering)
    Includes bibliographical references and index.
    ISBN 0-471-31641-5 (cloth : alk. paper)
    1. Options (Finance)   2. Hedging (Finance)   3. Foreign exchange
futures. I. Title. II. Series.
HG6024.A3D474   2000
332.64′5—dc21   99-38491

Printed in the United States of America
10   9   8   7   6   5   4   3   2   1

For Julia DeRosa

Contents

Preface

It is well known that foreign exchange is the world's largest financial market. What is less well known is that the market for currency options and other derivatives on foreign exchange is also massively large and still growing. Currency options are less visible than are options on other financial instruments because they trade mainly in the private interbank market. Sadly, the field of foreign exchange is not popular with authors of technical business books. The attention given to foreign exchange pales in comparison to the vast outpouring of books on the bond and stock markets.

This book has been written for end users of currency options and newcomers to the field of foreign exchange. I employ the real-world terminology of the foreign exchange market whenever possible so that readers can make a smooth transition from the text to actual market practice. *Options on Foreign Exchange* has a great many equations, but the level of mathematical difficulty seldom exceeds that of a first-semester course in differential calculus.

I use this book as the textbook for a course at the Yale School of Management entitled "Foreign Exchange and Its Related Derivative Instruments." I taught a forerunner of this course at the Graduate School of Business of the University of Chicago in 1995–1996. Students may be interested in a companion volume to this book that I edited for John Wiley & Sons. That book, *Currency Derivatives*, is a collection of scientific articles that have had an important impact on the development of the market for derivatives on foreign exchange. Risk managers may be interested in my *Managing Foreign Exchange Risk*, revised edition (1996).

The first edition of *Options on Foreign Exchange* came out in 1992. Since that time, the field has changed considerably, so I was keen to accept John Wiley & Sons' invitation to do a second edition. There are two major differences between this book and its first edition. This edition frames the discussion almost entirely in terms of currency options that trade in the interbank market, as opposed to the listed options and futures options markets. This change mirrors the migration of the currency option market from the listed environment of organized exchanges to the interbank foreign exchange market. Second, this edition pays a great deal more attention to exotic currency options, especially to barrier currency options.

David DeRosa
(*www.derosa-research.com*)

Acknowledgments

I wish to acknowledge the assistance of Hans Hsu, Delia Wang, Edward Pla, Allan Malz, David Lerman, Robert Sinche, Anne Pankowski, Joseph Leitch, David Johnson, Peter Halle, Ray Pullaro, Ashraf Rizvi, Steve Youngren, and Yuewu Xu. I extend special thanks for editorial assistance to Tommy Barron and Eduardo Mazzi. I am indebted to my friend Nassim Taleb for valued intellectual discussions. What errors that may remain are entirely my fault.

I would like to extend my gratitude to Montgomery Investment Technology Inc. for allowing me to use its software to prepare some of the exhibits in this book. I also thank Copp Clarke Professional and Mr. R. H. Lavers for permission to reprint a page of the Euromarket Dayfinder Calendar and EBS Dealing Resources, Inc. for permission to publish an image of a dealing screen. The RiskMetrics Group (*www.riskmetrics.com*) kindly supplied me with exchange rate and option volatility data.

David DeRosa

Options on Foreign Exchange

Second Edition

Chapter 1

Introduction to the Currency Option Market

The topic of this book is the specialized area of options on foreign exchange. Attention will be focused on plain-vanilla European puts and calls on foreign exchange as well as on some of the more popular exotic varieties of currency options.

Commercial and investment banks run the currency option market. The same money-center dealers that constitute the core of the spot and forward foreign exchange market are the most powerful market makers of currency options. For this reason, this book generally uses the conventions and terminology of the interbank foreign exchange option market.

Currency options are used by currency hedgers, traders, speculators, portfolio managers, and, on occasion, central banks.

History and Size of the Market

Trading in currency options began in the 1970s and 1980s in the venue of the listed futures and options markets of Chicago, Philadelphia, and London. Trading was concentrated in options and futures options on only a handful of major exchange rates. A structural change occurred in the 1990s, when the bulk of trading in currency options migrated "upstairs" to bank dealing rooms, to the detriment of the organized exchanges.

Once installed in the domain of the interbank foreign exchange market, option trading exploded in volume. What is more, currency options began to key off of the full gamut of exchange rates. In the mid 1990s, trading in exotic currency options began to develop at a rapid pace. Today, dealers routinely supply two-way bid-ask prices for a wide spectrum of exotic currency options. However, the largest appetites for exotic currency options are for barrier options. The market for basket options, average rate currency options, compound currency options, and quantos options is smaller, yet not insignificant.

The currency option market can rightfully claim to be the world's only truly global, 24-hour option market. The currency option market is among the largest of the option markets by trading volume. It is impossible to be precise about its overall size because the majority of trading in currency options is done in the private interbank market. But some rough estimates are reported in a survey done by the Bank for International Settlements (BIS). The most recent BIS survey estimated that the daily volume of currency option trading was $86.9 billion in face value in April 1998. Notable is that the number was only $41.2 billion when the same survey was done in April 1995.

The BIS survey reported that the largest portions of currency option trading are done in U.S. dollar/Japanese yen and the German mark (against a variety of currencies). In January 1999, the launch of the first round of the European Monetary Union meant that the new common currency, the euro, began to replace the German mark in foreign exchange derivatives trading.

Option Basics

The underlying asset for currency options is foreign exchange. The elementary foreign exchange transaction, called a spot deal, is a contract to deliver and receive sums of foreign currency for value in two bank business days.

Foreign exchange also trades on forward basis for value beyond the spot value date. Forward deals are routinely transacted for settlement on future spot value dates in one week, one month, three months, six months, and one year. The market exchange rate for forward dealing is called the forward outright.

Currency options are calls and puts on sums of foreign currency. They are the right but not the obligation to buy or sell a sum of currency at a fixed strike price on or before the option's expiration date.

Consider the following option on dollar/yen:

USD call/JPY put

Face amount in dollars	$10,000,000
Option put/call	Yen put
Option expiry	90 days
Strike	120.00
Exercise	European

This option is a call option on the U.S. dollar (USD) or equivalently, a put option on the Japanese yen (JPY). It grants its owner the right but not the obligation to receive $10,000,000 in exchange for delivery of 1,200,000,000 yen ($10 million × 120.00) at option expiration. This is an example of a standard, or *vanilla*, currency option.

European exercise means that an option can be exercised only on the last day of its life. Upon exercise, a currency option triggers a spot foreign exchange transaction done at the strike price and for settlement on the spot value date.

Barring exceptional circumstances, this option should be exercised if the spot exchange rate is above 120.00 on the expiration date. Likewise, a USD put/JPY call struck at the 120.00 should be exercised at expiration if the spot exchange rate is below 120.00. Interbank currency options can be transacted at practically any strike, but the most popular exercise price is at the prevailing forward outright (this is called *at-the-money-forward*).

European exercise currency options are surprisingly well understood using a simple adaptation of the Black-Scholes option-pricing model. In fact, Black-Scholes concepts and terminology permeate the currency option market. Option prices are quoted not in terms of dollars and cents but rather in units of Black-Scholes implied volatility. Currency options themselves are identified by their Black-Scholes delta more frequently than by their actual strike price. Moreover, Black-Scholes concepts, like delta, gamma, theta, and vega, have become the basic vocabulary of option risk management.

Although the great mass of interbank currency options is European exercise, there are some American exercise currency options. By definition, an American exercise option can be exercised at any time in its life. American exercise currency options can be priced with the binomial option-pricing model and also with a variety of numerical approximation techniques.

Exotic Options

An exotic currency option is an option that has some nonstandard feature that sets it apart from ordinary vanilla currency options. The foreign exchange market is a fertile ground for the invention of new exotic options.

The most popular exotic currency option is the barrier option. One type of barrier option is the *knock-out* option. A knock-out option is similar to a vanilla option except for the existence of a barrier exchange rate, called the *out-strike*, which when breached would cause the option to extinguish at any time during the option's life. For example, one could add an out-strike at 115.00 to the previously mentioned USD call/JPY put. This would mean that if dollar/yen were to trade at 115.00 before expiration, the option would cease to exist. Naturally, this option must cost less than its vanilla counterpart, which cannot be knocked out regardless of where dollar/yen trades.

There are also *double-barrier currency options*, which can be extinguished by either of two out-strikes.

A *binary option* pays a lump sum of cash if the option is in-the-money at expiration. Binary options too can have one or two barrier out-strikes.

Another exotic binary option is the one-touch. This option pays a lump sum of cash to the holder of the option if its barrier level is traded. A special form of binary exotic option, called the *double-barrier range binary*, has caught the attention of the trading community. This option pays a lump sum of cash at expiration provided that no barrier event takes place in the option's life. Double-barrier range binary options are used in volatility trading.

Although barrier currency options are mainly popular with traders and speculators, other types of exotic currency options are favorites with foreign exchange risk managers. A *basket* option is a put or a call on the aggregate value of a portfolio of foreign currencies. Basket options are popular because they offer economical solutions for hedging foreign exchange risk. *Compound options* are options on options. When one acquires a compound call option, one has the right but not the obligation to buy a vanilla call or put for a fixed compound strike price. *Average rate currency options* are cheap compared to vanilla options because their payoff at expiration is a function not of a single observation of the spot exchange rate but rather of an average of the spot exchange rate over a period of time. Still another exotic option for hedgers is the *quantos* option. The quantos option has a floating face amount that adjusts to the market value of the underlying portfolio that is the subject of the hedging program.

Chapter **2**

Foreign Exchange Basics

This chapter introduces some basic knowledge about foreign exchange that the reader must have before tackling currency options.

The foreign exchange market does a phenomenal volume of trading. The most recent survey conducted by the Bank of International Settlements estimates that the volume of trading in the foreign exchange spot and forward markets totaled $1.490 trillion per day in April 1998. Trading in currencies is conducted in practically every large city of the world and the market is open 24 hours per day, except on weekends and holidays.

The International Monetary System

Bretton Woods and the Smithsonian Period

For the first quarter century after World War II, the international monetary system consisted of a program of fixed exchange rates. Fixed exchange rates were established under the Bretton Woods agreement signed by the Allied powers in 1944 in advance of the end of the war. The Bretton Woods agreement required all member central banks to keep their foreign exchange reserves in U.S. dollars, pounds sterling, or gold. More importantly, member countries agreed to stabilize their currencies within a ±1 percent band around a target rate of exchange to the U.S. dollar. The dollar, in turn, was pegged to gold bullion at $35 per ounce. The system lasted until 1973.

Periodically, currencies had to be revalued and devalued when market pressures became too great for central banks to oppose. Cynics dubbed Bretton Woods a "system of creeping pegs." In 1971, after a series of dramatic "dollar crises," the dollar was devalued against gold to $38 an ounce, and a wider band width, equal to ±2.25%, was established. This modification to the system, called the Smithsonian Agreement, postponed the collapse of the system of fixed exchange rates for two years. In 1973, the entire structure of fixed exchange rates that began with Bretton Woods was scrapped. Since that time, the dollar has not been pegged to gold, and exchange rates for major currencies against the dollar have been floating.

The Euro

On January 1, 1999, 11 European nation members of the European Monetary Union, Germany, Belgium, Luxembourg, Spain, France, Ireland, Italy, the Netherlands, Austria, Portugal, and Finland, adopted a new common currency, called the euro. The legacy currencies of these 11 nations, such as the German mark and French franc, circulate in parallel to the euro but are convertible to the euro at fixed exchange rates. Total conversion to the euro is planned to happen at some time before January 1, 2002, whereupon the European Central Bank will issue euro notes and coins that will irrevocably replace the legacy currencies. Additional European countries may choose to adopt the euro over time. Noteworthy by their absences in the first round of conversion to the euro are the United Kingdom, Denmark, and Greece. Switzerland is not part of the European Monetary Union.

The road to the creation of the euro was difficult. For nearly two decades, starting with the creation of the European Monetary System in March 1979, parts of Europe experimented with a fixed exchange rate system that was known as the Exchange Rate Mechanism (ERM). Under the ERM, member countries agreed to peg their currencies to a basket currency called the European Currency Unit (ECU). Currencies were allowed to move in relation to the ECU within either the narrow band of ±2.25 percent or the wide band of ±6 percent.

The ERM was a costly experiment in fixed exchange rate policy. In its 20 years of operation, from 1979 to 1999, ERM central rates had to be adjusted over 50 times. More spectacular yet were the two major ERM currency crises, one in September 1992 and the other in August 1993, each of which involved massive central bank losses in the defense of the fixed exchange rate grid. Finally, after the second crisis, fluctuation bands were widened to ±15 percent, a move that effectively neutered the ERM.

Fixed Exchange Rate Regimes

A great variety of fixed exchange rate regimes have come and gone in the twentieth century, especially with respect to the minor currencies and emerging market currencies. Only a handful of fixed exchange rate systems have been worth the trouble. One success story was the Austrian shilling, which remained faithfully pegged to the German mark for nearly 20 years before joining the ERM in January 1995.

But a great many other cases of fixed exchange rate regimes ended badly. History shows that pegged exchange rates are astonishingly explosive and damaging when they fail. The recent examples of the Mexican peso in 1994 and the Thai baht, Czech koruna, and Indonesian rupiah in 1997 are cases in point.

Fixed exchange rate regimes in their most simple form consist of a currency being pegged outright to the value of another currency. A few fixed exchange rate regimes are operated under the framework of a currency board, such as the ones that are in place in Hong Kong and Argentina. Under the workings of a currency board, the government commits to maintaining a reserve of foreign exchange equal to the outstanding domestic base money supply and to exchange domestic and foreign reserve currency at the pegged exchange rate on demand.

Basket peg systems are another fixed exchange rate regime. The Thai baht was operated as a basket peg currency before its spectacular collapse in July 1997. Under the basket regime, the Bank of Thailand pegged the baht to a basket of currencies made up of U.S. dollars, German marks, and Japanese yen, though the exact makeup of the basket was never revealed.

Another species of a fixed exchange rate regime pegs the currency but permits gradual depreciation over time. Examples are the Mexican peso prior to the December 1994 crisis and the Indonesian rupiah before it collapsed in July 1997.

Still other currencies fit somewhere between floating and pegged exchange rate regimes. Singapore, for example, operates what properly could be described as a "managed" floating regime.

Exchange Rate Intervention

Since the end of the Bretton Woods system in 1973, the value of the U.S. dollar against the currencies of America's major trading partners has been determined by the forces of free-market supply and demand. Yet that is an exaggeration because all exchange rates are subject to manipulation by governmental bodies.

Today, the major countries coordinate foreign exchange policy through the G-7 council. G-7 stands for the Group of Seven industrialized nations, which is composed of the United States, Japan, Canada, the United Kingdom, Italy, Germany, and France.

The council has periodically conducted interventions in the foreign exchange market through coordinated central bank buying and selling of currencies against the dollar. The most historically significant case of intervention by what was then known as the G-5 council surrounded the Plaza Accord in September 1985 (See Funabashi, 1989). At that time, the council decided that it should lower the value of the U.S. dollar. Accordingly, its member nations' central banks launched a massive program to sell the dollar. The Plaza maneuver is remembered in foreign exchange history as the most successful coordinated intervention; the dollar fell by more than 4 percent in the first 24 hours. Since that time, the council has been at times more concerned about the stability of the dollar than its level. This was the focus of the other historic council meeting at the Louvre in February 1997. The G-7 was active in foreign exchange markets throughout the first term of the Clinton presidency (1992–1996), when Secretaries of the Treasury Lloyd Bentsen and Robert Rubin organized numerous G-7 interventions to support the dollar.

Exchange Rate Crises

The Southeast Asian currencies experienced tremendous volatility in the summer of 1997. Two currencies, the Thai baht and the Indonesian rupiah, abandoned long-held fixed exchange rate regimes. The Malaysian ringgit and Philippine peso suffered steep losses in value against the U.S. dollar. The Korean won, a currency that was not fully convertible, also was devalued. One of the only convertible currencies in Asia not to be devalued was the Hong Kong dollar.

After the fact, basic macroeconomic analysis can explain this remarkable series of currency crises with a simple set of causal factors that relate to the fundamental domestic conditions in each of these countries. Many of the affected countries had banking systems that were on the verge of total breakdown before the exchange rate problems became manifest. Moreover, several countries were running enormous and unsustainable current account imbalances, and every one of the afflicted countries had managed to run up staggering foreign currency–denominated debts.

Nonetheless, in some quarters, the blame for the entire episode was put on hedge funds, currency speculators, and the generally mistaken notion that capital mobility invites disaster. No matter what one ultimately chooses to believe was the cause of the crisis or where one enjoys placing the blame, the Asian currency crisis of 1997–1998 clearly demonstrates that exchange rates are capable of making violent and substantial—if not outright discontinuous— movements over short periods of time.

Spot Foreign Exchange and Market Conventions[1]

Spot Foreign Exchange

Spot and forward foreign exchange is traded in the interbank market by money-center banks and investment banks that act as principal dealers. The most important locations for foreign exchange trading are London, New York, and Tokyo, though dealing rooms can be found in every important city in the world.

The spot exchange rate is a quotation for the exchange of currencies in two bank business days' time (except in the case of the Canadian dollar versus the U.S. dollar, where delivery is in one bank business day).

Foreign exchange settlement days are called *value dates.* To qualify as a value date, a day must not be a bank holiday in either currency's country and it must not be a bank holiday in the United States. Many traders rely on a special calendar called the Euromarket Day Finder Calendar, published by Copp Clark Professional, to find value dates and identify international holidays. A sample page of this calendar for trade date August 27, 1998, is displayed in Exhibit 2.1. Note that the value date for spot transactions in dollar/mark for trade August 27 would be August 31. However,

---

1. Legal definitions of the vocabulary of foreign exchange dealing can be found in the *1998 FX and Currency Option Definitions,* published by the International Swaps and Derivatives Association (New York, 1998).

Thursday

27

August 1998

SUN	MON	TUE	WED	THU	FRI	SAT
						1 Z
2	3 AT	4	5	6	7	8
9	10 S	11	12	13	14	15 MP
16	17 H	18	19	20	21	22
23	24	25	26	27	28 1	29
30	31 ■					

July 1998

S	M	T	W	T	F	S
			1	2	3	4
5	6	7	8	9	10	11
12	13	14	15	16	17	18
19	20	21	22	23	24	25
26	27	28	29	30	31	

239
Day Number

126
Days Remaining

★ New York
● Tokyo
■ London
▲ Frankfurt
▦ Lunar New Year

H Hong Kong
M Milan
P Paris
S Singapore
A Sydney/Melbourne
T Toronto
W Wellington
Z Zurich

❶ Sep 98

S	M	T	W	T	F	S
	1 5	2 6	3 7	4 8	5	
6	7 ★	8 12	9 13	10 14	11 15	12
13	14 18	15 ●	16 20	17 21	18 22	19
20	21 25	22 26	23 ●	24 28	25 29	26
27	32	29 33	30 34			

❷ Oct 98

S	M	T	W	T	F	S
				1 35	2 36	3 ▲
4	5 39	6 40	7 41	8 42	9 43	10 ●
11	12 ★	13 47	14 48	15 49	16 50	17
18	19 53	20 54	21 55	22 56	23 57	24
25	26 60	61	28 62	29 63	30 64	31

❸ Nov 98

S	M	T	W	T	F	S
1	2 67	3 ●	4 69	5 70	6 71	7
8	9 74	10 75	11 ★	12 77	13 78	14
15	16 81	17 82	18 83	19 84	20 85	21
22	23 ●	24 89	25 90	26 ★	92	28
29	30 95					

❹ Dec 98

S	M	T	W	T	F	S
	1 96	2 97	3 98	4 99	5	
6	7 102	8 103	9 104	10 105	11 106	12
13	14 109	15 110	16 111	17 112	18 113	19
20	21 116	22 117	23 ●	24	★	26 ■▲
27		29 124	30 125	31 ●		

❺ Jan 99

S	M	T	W	T	F	S
					★● ■▲	2 ●
3 ●	4 130	5 131	6 132	7 133	8 134	9
10	11 137	12 138	13 139	14 140	15 ●	16
17	18 ★	19 145	20 146	21 147	22 148	23
24	25 151	26 152	153	28 154	29 155	30
31						

❻ Feb 99

S	M	T	W	T	F	S
	1 158	2 159	3 160	4 161	5 162	6
7	8 165	9 166	10 167	11 ●	12 169	13
14	15 ★	16 173	17 174	18 175	19 176	20
21	22 179	23 180	24 181	25 182	183	27
28						

Swaps/Mid-term table

THIS DATE IN

1. 1999 is a Friday
2. 2000 is a **Sunday**
3. 2001 is a **Monday** ■
4. 2002 is a Tuesday
5. 2003 is a Wednesday
6. 2004 is a Friday
7. 2005 is a **Saturday**
8. 2006 is a **Sunday**
9. 2007 is a **Monday** ■
10. 2008 is a Wednesday

Count-back table

TO DETERMINE
THE NUMBER OF DAYS
BACK FROM TODAY,
DEDUCT DATES IN

Jul **98** from	58	Jan **98** from	239
Jun **98** from	88	Dec **97** from	270
May **98** from	119	Nov **97** from	300
Apr **98** from	149	Oct **97** from	331
Mar **98** from	180	Sep **97** from	361
Feb **98** from	208	Aug **97** from	392

Swaps/Mid-term table

THIS DATE IN

11. 2009 is a Thursday
12. 2010 is a Friday
13. 2011 is a **Saturday**
14. 2012 is a **Monday** ■
15. 2013 is a Tuesday
16. 2014 is a Wednesday
17. 2015 is a Thursday
18. 2016 is a **Saturday**
19. 2017 is a **Sunday**
20. 2018 is a **Monday** ■

THU 27 AUG 1998   ©Copp Clark Professional & R.H. Lavers   **EUROMARKET DAY FINDER®**

Exhibit 2.1   Euromarket Dayfinder Calendar. Reprinted with permission.

Thu 27 Aug 1998

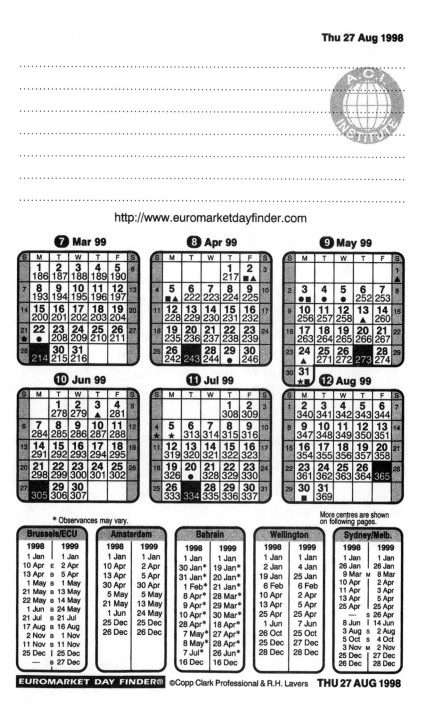

http://www.euromarketdayfinder.com

* Observances may vary.

More centres are shown on following pages.

Brussels/ECU		Amsterdam		Bahrain		Wellington		Sydney/Melb.	
1998	1999	1998	1999	1998	1999	1998	1999	1998	1999
1 Jan	1 Jan	1 Jan	1 Jan	1 Jan	1 Jan	1 Jan	1 Jan	1 Jan	1 Jan
10 Apr E	2 Apr	10 Apr	2 Apr	30 Jan*	19 Jan*	2 Jan	4 Jan	26 Jan	26 Jan
13 Apr B	5 Apr	13 Apr	5 Apr	31 Jan*	20 Jan*	19 Jan	25 Jan	9 Mar M	8 Mar
1 May B	1 May	30 Apr	30 Apr	1 Feb*	21 Jan*	6 Feb	6 Feb	10 Apr	2 Apr
21 May B	13 May	5 May	5 May	8 Apr*	28 Mar*	10 Apr	2 Apr	11 Apr	3 Apr
22 May B	14 May	21 May	13 May	9 Apr*	29 Mar*	13 Apr	5 Apr	13 Apr	5 Apr
1 Jun B	24 May	1 Jun	24 May	10 Apr*	30 Mar*	25 Apr	25 Apr	25 Apr	25 Apr
21 Jul B	21 Jul	25 Dec	25 Dec	28 Apr*	18 Apr*	1 Jun	7 Jun	— s	26 Apr
17 Aug B	16 Aug	26 Dec	26 Dec	7 May*	27 Apr*	26 Oct	25 Oct	8 Jun	14 Jun
2 Nov B	1 Nov			8 May*	28 Apr*	25 Dec	27 Dec	3 Aug s	2 Aug
11 Nov B	11 Nov			7 Jul*	26 Jun*	28 Dec	28 Dec	5 Oct s	4 Oct
25 Dec I	25 Dec			16 Dec	16 Dec			3 Nov M	2 Nov
— B	27 Dec							25 Dec	27 Dec
								26 Dec	28 Dec

EUROMARKET DAY FINDER®   ©Copp Clark Professional & R.H. Lavers   **THU 27 AUG 1998**

Exhibit 2.1   *Continued.*

the value date for spot sterling deals would be September 1 because August 31 is a London holiday (called the "summer bank holiday").

The foreign exchange week commences at 6 A.M. Sydney time, when New Zealand and Australian dealers open the market on Monday morning. Later, Tokyo, Singapore, and Hong Kong join the fray to constitute the Austral-Asian dealing time zone. Next, the center of the market shifts to London as it opens, but Frankfurt, Paris, Milan, Madrid, and Zurich also conduct a sizable amount of currency dealing. New York is the capital of foreign exchange dealing in the Western Hemisphere. At 5 P.M. New York time, trading seamlessly advances to the next value day.

Quotation Conventions

Dealers make spot exchange rate quotations as bid-ask quotations. For example, a quote on the dollar/yen of 125.00/125.10 means that a dealer is willing to buy dollars and sell yen at the rate of 125.00 yen per dollar or sell dollars and buy yen at the rate of 125.10 yen per dollar. A *pip* is defined as the smallest unit of quotation for a currency. Therefore, a quote on dollar/yen of 125.00/125.10 is said to be 10 pips wide.

To this day, almost all currency trading is done against the dollar. Backing up that remarkable fact is the 1998 survey of the foreign exchange trading done by the BIS that estimated that the dollar was on one side of 87 percent of all foreign exchange deals. A notable exception in the 1998 survey was direct trading of currencies against the German mark. The most important of the so-called mark "crosses" was mark/yen and sterling/mark.

Currency trading is a fast-moving business. Dealing rooms are crowded, noisy, and stress-filled environments. For that reason, the foreign exchange community has developed rules on how quotations and trading instructions are given. The most basic rule is that the first currency in an exchange rate pair is the direct object of the trade. To buy 10 million dollar/yen is to buy 10 million dollars against yen. The hierarchy for major exchange rates is as follows:

EUR	Euro
GBP	Sterling
USD	Dollar
Non-euro	European national currencies
JPY	Japanese yen

The rule in the professional market is that the higher currency on the grid is the one that deals. For example, the euro deals against all currencies (EUR/GBP; EUR/USD; EUR/JPY).

Unfortunately, two conventions for the quotation of spot foreign exchange have evolved. In the American convention, currency is quoted in terms of U.S. dollars per unit of foreign exchange (for example, sterling quoted at 1.7000 means that it takes 1.7000 U.S. dollars to equal one pound). The pound, Australian dollar, New Zealand dollar, and the euro are quoted American. Other currencies are quoted European, which means they are expressed in the number of units of foreign exchange equal to one U.S. dollar (i.e., 120.00 yen per one U.S. dollar or 1.6500 marks per one dollar).

The advent of the euro represents a challenge to foreign exchange trading conventions. As has been noted, the euro trades American convention (i.e., EUR/USD) against the dollar. However, the European Central Bank has decided to permit trading in the European legacy currencies at least until the year 2002, but conversions must be done at fixed exchange rates. The euro fixing rates against the legacy currencies (Exhibit 2.2) and the fixing rates for trading between the legacy currencies (Exhibit 2.3) were locked on December 31, 1998. One more matter that makes things even more confusing is that most exchange-traded currency futures and options quote currencies American, even for currencies that are quoted European in the spot market.

German mark	DEM	1.955583
Belgian franc	BEF	40.339900
Luxembourg franc	LUF	40.339900
Spanish peseta	ESP	166.386000
French franc	FRF	6.559570
Irish punt	IEP	0.787564
Italian lira	ITL	1936.270000
Dutch guilder	NLG	2.203710
Austrian schilling	ATS	13.760300
Portuguese escudo	PTE	200.482000
Finnish markka	FIM	5.945730

Exhibit 2.2 Euro fixing rates—official fixing rates versus euro as of December 31, 1998.

	DEM (100)	BEF/LUF (100)	ESP (100)	FRF (100)	IEP (1)	ITL (1,000)	NLG (100)	ATS (1,000)	PTE (100)	FIM (1)
DEM	—									
BEF/LUF	2062.55	—								
ESP	8507.22	412.462	—							
FRF	335.386	16.2608	3.94237	—						
IEP	40.2676	1.95232	0.473335	12.0063	—					
ITL	99000.2	4799.90	1163.72	29518.3	2458.56	—				
NLG	112.674	5.46285	1.32445	33.5953	2.79812	1.13812	—			
ATS	703.552	34.1108	8.27006	209.774	17.4719	7.10657	624.415	—		
PTE	10250.5	496.984	120.492	3056.34	254.560	103.541	9097.53	1456.97	—	
FIM	304.001	14.7391	3.57345	90.6420	7.54951	3.07071	269.806	43.2094	2.96571	—

Exhibit 2.3 EMS irrevocable bilateral rates, December 31, 1998.

Settlement of Foreign Exchange Trades

Interbank spot foreign exchange transactions settle on value date with the physical exchange of sums of currencies. Every foreign exchange deal results in a cross-border transaction in the sense that settlement involves the transfer of bank deposits in two countries. If Bank A buys 10 million euros against dollars from Bank B at the rate of 1.1700, on value day, Bank A will receive 10 million euros from Bank B in a Frankfurt account. On the same day, Bank B will receive 11.7 million dollars from Bank A in a New York account.

Hypothetically, suppose that a customer of a certain dealing bank is "bullish" on dollar/yen. The customer asks for a quote from the bank on the size of 10 million dollars. Bank A quotes the customer 115.00-05. The customer buys 10 million dollars at 115.05. This takes place in the New York morning trading session and by the afternoon, the dollar has risen. When the dollar is trading at the 116.00 level, the customer decides to liquidate the position to realize his profit. The customer solicits a quote and the bank "makes him" 116.10-15. The customer sells his dollars at 116.10.

The customer could settle the transaction and realize the profit in either dollars or yen. The initial transaction created a long position of 10 million dollars and a short position of 1,150,500,000 yen. If the customer did the second transaction to sell exactly 10 million dollars, the profit would consist of the residual 10,500,000 yen. If the customer wanted the profit in dollars, he could tell the dealer to sell exactly 1,150,500,000 yen at the dealer's price of 116.10. This would leave the client with a profit equal to $90,439.28 and most certainly a cause for celebration.

But not all foreign exchange deals are settled with physical exchange of currency, especially with non–bank customer trades. Most dealing banks offer their customers the convenience of settling on the basis of the net profit or loss on a deal.

Foreign Exchange Dealing

Two-Way Prices

Foreign exchange dealers stand ready to make bid-ask quotes on potentially very large amounts of currency to customers as well as to other banks. There is a distinction in the interbank market between reciprocal and nonreciprocal trading relationships. In a reciprocal trading relationship, two banks agree to supply each other with *two-way* (i.e., bid-ask) quotations on demand. Reciprocal trading relationships between money-center banks constitute the core of the foreign exchange market. A nonreciprocal trading relationship is merely a customer trading facility that happens to be between a small bank and a large money-center dealing bank. The dealer agrees to quote foreign exchange to the smaller bank, but the reverse never is expected to happen.

It is the custom in the foreign exchange market for the party soliciting a quote to reveal the size of the transaction at its onset. For example, someone might ask a dealer for "dollar/yen on 10," meaning a bid-ask quote on 10 million dollars. For large orders, say anything above 100 million dollars in a major currency (but less than that in a minor currency), the dealer might inquire whether the order is the *full amount*. If the party indicates that the order is indeed the full amount, it means that the indicated size will not be immediately followed by similar transactions of the customer's own initiation. Why would it matter to the dealer? The answer is that under usual circumstances, the dealer will seek to rebalance its dealing book once a customer order is filled. For example, if the customer buys 100 million dollars against yen, then the dealing bank would be left short dollars and would immediately be in the market, buying dollars, using its reciprocal trading counterparties. The problem with a non–full amount order is that it could put the customer and the dealer in competition in the aftermarket when the dealer is trying to reconstitute its book from the effect of the original customer transaction.

Limit Orders and Stop-Loss Orders

Foreign exchange dealers accept *limit orders* and *stop-loss orders*. A limit order gives a precise price at which a customer is willing to buy or sell foreign exchange. A stop-loss order is a more complicated instruction. Stop-loss orders are designed to liquidate bad trades in a timely manner so as to avoid steep losses. A trader who bought dollar/yen at 115.00 might leave instructions to be "stopped out" at 113.50. Banks accept stop-loss orders only on a best-efforts basis.

This means that there is no guarantee that any stop-loss order will be executed exactly at the stop level, in this case at 113.50.

Stop orders present dealers with a chance to make some serious money if they are able to get the feel of the market correctly. Say that when dollar/yen is trading at 114.00, a customer gives a dealer a stop order to liquidate a position of long 10 million dollars at 113.50. Suppose that the dollar falls to the 113.70 level. If the dealer has a good hunch that it will still go lower and trade at the 113.50 level, he will sell 10 million dollars immediately for his own account in anticipation of being able to fill the customer's stop-loss order later, when 113.50 trades. If 113.50 in fact does trade, the dealer will have a profit of 20 pips, equal to the difference between where he sold dollars for his own account (at 113.70) and where he bought dollars (at 113.50) from the customer to fill the stop-loss order. This trick is not without risk, however. Consider that the dealer could have sold dollars at 113.70 only to see the dollar rebound upward, leaving him short dollars in a rising market and unable to fill the customer's stop-loss order.

Knowledge of the placement of limit orders and stop-loss orders, collectively called the *order board*, is valuable information for the dealer. Sometimes the order board for a large dealer yields clues as to near-term movement of currencies. Stop-loss orders can cause sudden, large movements in exchange rates, especially in cases where the market runs past an important level where there are large quantities of unfilled stop-loss orders. Nonetheless, there is no getting around the need for stop-loss orders.

In recent years, stop-loss orders have become a larger factor in the foreign exchange market because of the growing popularity of exotic options. Exotic option risk management for dealers and customers often depends on efficient execution of stop-loss orders.

Direct Dealing and Brokers

Foreign exchange dealers communicate with each other through computer messaging services. Each dealer has the ability to conduct a brief text conversation with his or her counterparts at other dealing banks for the purpose of conducting foreign exchange trading. The actual text of a foreign exchange dealer conversation is usually highly abbreviated and assumes a close knowledge of market conditions. Exhibit 2.4 shows a hypothetical foreign exchange deal.

Dealers make prices directly to other foreign exchange dealing banks but sometimes use the assistance of specialized foreign exchange brokers. *Voice* brokers work exclusively with the interbank market. They communicate with their client dealing banks via private direct phone lines. At all times, the job of the voice broker is to know who is making the highest bid and lowest ask for each currency. Brokers work their clients' orders in strict confidence, never revealing the name of a dealing bank until a trade has been completed. Brokers supply an important function in the foreign exchange market in that they collect and distribute price information.

In recent years the voice brokers have suffered from competition from the Electronic Broking System (EBS). EBS is owned by a partnership of the money-center banks. Since its launch in 1993, the EBS Spot Dealing System has captured a significant share of the global foreign exchange spot broking market.

EBS Spot Dealing is a screen-based anonymous dealing system for spot trading, in all major currencies, delivered over a proprietary electronic network. The EBS Spot Dealing System integrates spot dealing with bank-assigned counterparty credit facilities. Dealers see only bids and asks that are supplied from counterparties for whom they have available dealing lines.

A sample EBS screen is shown in Exhibit 2.5. It is worth taking a look at the components of the screen:

Price Panel/Multiple Currency Trading

The EBS multiple currency displays current bids and asks on up to six currency pairs simultaneously. Euro/dollar is quoted at 1.1199–1.1201 on the top of the panel. All prices that are supplied are prescreened for credit.

Credit Information

The pretrade credit screening and warning panels indicate when a counterparty is approaching its predetermined credit limit or has reached its limit.

```
EUR/USD SPOT SELL @ 1.1545 10 MIO EPSF EPICENTER SF REVW
 1 EUR 10
 2 40  45
 3 I BUY
 4 VALUE 6JAN1999
 5 TO CONFIRM 10 MIO AGREED AT 1.1545 I SELL EUR
 6 MY USD TO ABCBANK, NY
 7 THANKS AND BYE
 8 TO CONFIRM AT 1.1545 I BUY 10 MIO EUR
 9 VALUE 6JAN1999
10 MY EUR TO EPICENTER BANK, LONDON
11 THANKS AND BYE
```

Explanation

Line 1:   EpiCenter Bank calls ABCBank to ask for a quote on 10 million euro/USD.

Line 2:   ABCBank offers to buy euros against dollars at 1.1540 and sell euros against dollars at 1.1545. The "handle" 1.15 is assumed.

Line 3:   EpiCenter buys euros against dollars at 1.1545.

Line 4–7:   ABCBank confirms the trade and the value date and instructs EpiCenter to deliver dollars to ABCBank New York.

Lines 8–11: EpiCenter confirms the trade and the value date and instructs ABCBank to deliver euros to EpiCenter Bank in London.

Exhibit 2.4   A hypothetical foreign exchange dealing conversation (EpiCenter Bank of California, San Francisco Branch, EPSF and ABCBank New York).

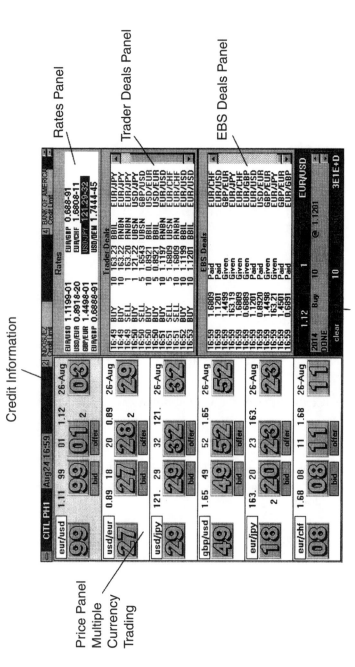

Exhibit 2.5 Sample EBS screen. *Source:* EBS Dealing Resources, Inc. Reprinted with permission.

Rates Panel

Bids and asks are displayed real-time.

EBS Deals Panel

All trades executed over EBS are listed on the EBS deals panel, indicating activity in given markets. The deals marked "given" indicate that the bank initiating the trade was a seller of the base currency; deals marked "paid" mean that the bank initiating the trade was a buyer of the base currency.

Trader Deals

The trader deals panel displays summary information on a dealer's complete deals for the current day.

Transaction Status Panel

This panel provides dealers with immediate feedback as to the status of a transaction once it is submitted to the EBS Spot Market. Note that the trader has just been informed that he has bought 10 million euros against dollars at the rate of 1.1201.

Interest Parity and Forward Foreign Exchange

The Forward Outright

A forward exchange rate is a quotation for settlement or value on a date in the future beyond the spot value date. Forward rates can be negotiated for any valid future spot value date, but indications are usually given for one week, one month, three months, six months, and one year in the future. The Euromarket Day Finder Calendar (Exhibit 2.1) is the customary arbiter of what is or is not a valid forward value date.

The forward exchange rate, called the *outright,* is usually quoted in two parts, one being the spot bid or ask, and the other a two-way quote on forward points. Forward points are either added or subtracted from the spot rate to arrive at the forward outright.

Suppose that spot dollar yen is 114.83/88 and that three-month forward points are quoted −139/−135. Forward points are always quoted in foreign exchange pips. Forward points in this case are subtracted from the spot level to obtain the three-month outright:

Dealer's bid	*Dealer's ask*
114.83	114.88
−1.39	−1.35
113.44	113.53

Interest Parity

When the preceding example was created, forward points for the yen happened to be negative because yen interest rates were below dollar interest rates. Had the yen interest rates been above dollar rates, the forward points would have been positive in sign. This relationship between spot exchange rates, forward points, and interest rates is called the *covered interest parity theorem*. This theorem explains forward exchange rates, and it plays an important role in currency option theory.

The basic concept is that the market sets forward rates in relation to spot in order to absorb the interest rate spread between two currencies. It is a no-free-lunch idea: One cannot hop between currencies, picking up yield advantage, and lock up a guaranteed profit by using the forward market to hedge against currency risk. The forward outright acts as the equalizer.

For example, suppose a Japanese yen–based investor is attracted by comparatively higher yields in U.S. dollar instruments. Suppose that the yield on one-year yen paper is 0.75 percent, the yield on one-year dollar paper is 5.25 percent, and the spot dollar/yen is equal to 115.00.

The Japanese investor might consider converting yen to dollars for the purpose of investing in high-yielding dollar paper. Parenthetically, this is the raison d'etre for a whole host of strategies known as yen-carry trades. The problem is that there is no way for the investor to capture some of the yield spread between the dollar and the yen without taking risk on the future direction of the spot exchange rate. If the dollar were to subsequently decline against the yen, some or all of the prospective yield pickup would be lost. If the dollar were to fall sufficiently, there might be a net capital loss on the transaction. On the other hand, if the dollar were to rise, the investor would make a profit to an extent greater than the indicated yield spread of 450 basis points.

Hedging cannot get around the problem. Consider that the investor might contemplate hedging the foreign exchange risk by selling forward the future value of the dollars invested in the United States versus the yen. The key question is what forward rate for dollar/yen would be available in the marketplace. The only forward rate that makes sense from an overall market perspective is 110.083. Any other forward outright implies that riskless arbitrage would be possible. To see this, suppose that the investor starts out with 100 million yen. If the investor buys one-year yen paper, the sum would grow to 100,750,000 yen. On the other hand, if the investor converts the yen to dollars, the investor would receive $869,565.22. Invested for one year in dollar paper, the sum would grow to $915,217.40. The only arbitrage-free forward outright is then

$$\frac{100,750,000}{915,217.40} = 110.083$$

At this forward rate, the investor would be indifferent between dollar-denominated paper and yen-denominated paper on a fully hedged basis.

Denote the current time as t and the maturity date of the investment as T. The time remaining to maturity will be denoted as τ, which is equal to

$$\tau = (T - t)$$

The covered interest parity theorem can be written in terms of either American or European convention:

Interest Parity: American Convention

$$F = S\frac{(1 + R_d)^\tau}{(1 + R_f)^\tau}$$

Interest Parity: European Convention

$$F' = S'\frac{(1 + R_f)^\tau}{(1 + R_d)^\tau}$$

F is the forward rate quoted American convention for settlement at time T, S is the spot rate quoted American, R_d is the domestic interest rate, and R_f is the foreign interest rate. F' and S' are the forward and spot rates quoted European convention. Both the domestic and foreign interest rates are simple interest rates in this formulation, but a more useful mathematical form can be had from working in terms of continuously compounded rates:

Interest Parity: American Convention

$$F = Se^{(R_d - R_f)\tau}$$

Interest Parity: European Convention

$$F' = S'e^{(R_f - R_d)\tau}$$

Specialized Forward Transactions

Dealers and other traders use the forward market to postpone, or *roll*, a maturing foreign exchange deal out on the calendar to a future value date. Two specialized forward transactions that accomplish this purpose are the *spot/next* and *tom/next swap deals*. They are best understood in the context of an original spot foreign exchange deal. Suppose a trader buys 10 million euros against dollars spot at 1.1700. Spot transactions are for value in two bank business days.

Suppose that on the deal day, the trader decides to extend the value date by one day. She could accomplish this by doing a spot/next swap transaction. A spot/next deal is actually a package of two trades that are bundled together. In the first part of the swap, the trader sells 10 million euros against dollars for normal spot value (hence the "spot"). Simultaneously, the trader buys 10 million euros against dollars for tomorrow's spot value date (hence the "next"). This accomplishes the stated goal of delaying settlement by one day because the settlement from the original spot deal crosses and is the opposite direction to the settlement in the first component of the spot/next swap. Some residual cash flows may yet occur on the original spot value date because of movements in the spot exchange rate between the time that the spot deal is made and when the spot/next roll is executed. Ordinarily this would be small in magnitude unless a violent movement in exchange rates has taken place.

Tom/next is practically the same thing as spot/next except that it is done on the day following the original spot deal (deal date plus one day). Continuing with the example, in the "tom" part of the trade, the trader sells 10 million euros for dollars for value "tomorrow." Tomorrow corresponds to the original deal's value date, which makes the settlement deliveries cross each other. The second part of the tom/next is a spot transaction to buy 10 million euros against dollars for the "next" value date—meaning the regular spot value date in two bank business days.

Either way, using spot/next or tom/next, the trader in the example is able to maintain a long position in 10 million euro/dollar for one extra day without having to make physical delivery of the underlying sums of currency. Theoretically, the trader could continue to roll the value date using spot/next or tom/next transactions and keep the position on for an indefinite time. Alternatively, a trader could roll the position out for more than one day by doing a single swap transaction of spot against a forward outright for a specific term in the future. Squeezes in spot/next and tom/next are notorious but actually not that common in occurrence. Yet emerging market central banks have been known to engineer squeezes to flush speculators from taking or maintaining short positions in their currency.

Nondeliverable Forward Transactions

Forward transactions can be done on a nondeliverable basis. In a nondeliverable forward (NDF), counterparties agree to settle a forward transaction with the payment of a settlement amount payable on the forward value date. The fixing date is defined as two bank business days before the forward value date. The fixing rate is defined as the observed spot exchange rate posted by a central bank on the fixing date. Settlement amount is defined as

$$Settlement\ amount = Notional - \left[\frac{Notional \times Forward\ Outright}{Fixing\ rate} \right]$$

where the notional amount is another term for the forward face amount.

Nondeliverable forwards are essential for trading in currencies that are not fully convertible because delivery of physical currency may not be feasible. Sometimes NDF markets spontaneously spring up in cases where a government suspends currency convertibility or enacts capital controls, as did Malaysia in 1997.

Chapter **3**

Trading Currency Options

This chapter covers the mechanics of trading currency options. The largest market for currency option trading is the interbank market, although there is also active trading in listed currency options on the Philadelphia Stock Exchange and listed currency futures options on the Chicago Mercantile Exchange.

The Interbank Currency Option Market

A currency put confers the right, but not the obligation, to sell a sum of foreign currency to the option seller (called the *writer*) at a fixed exchange rate called the *option strike* on or before the option expiration. A currency call confers the right but not the obligation to buy a sum of foreign currency from the option writer at the option strike on or before the option expiration.

A call option on one currency is simultaneously a put option on a second currency. An unambiguous but somewhat redundant method identifies currency options by referring to both of the involved currencies. For example, the options in Exhibit 3.1 are referred to as a USD call/JPY put—referred to as a yen put—and a USD put/JPY call—referred to as a yen call. USD and JPY are the interbank codes for the U.S. dollar and the Japanese yen, respectively.

The interbank market is also home to a wide variety of exotic currency options, some of which are discussed in Chapters 9 and 10.

Face Values

The face value of each option is $10,000,000 in Exhibit 3.1. The options are struck at dollar/yen equal to 114.58. The face value of the options in yen can be found by multiplying the face in dollars by the strike, which is equal to 1,145,800,000 yen.

Currency pair	USD/JPY	USD/JPY
Put/Call	USD put/JPY call	USD call/JPY put
Face USD	$10,000,000	$10,000,000
Face JPY	1,145,800,000	1,145,800,000
Strike	114.58	114.58
Days to expiry	30	30
Market data		
Spot	115.00	115.00
Forward outright	114.58	114.58
Option pricing		
USD pips	0.00020195	0.00020195
Total USD	$231,394	$231,394
JPY pips (4 digits)	2.6610	2.6610
Total JPY	26,610,000	26,610,000
Percentage of face amount	2.31%	2.31%

Exhibit 3.1   Vanilla European currency option pricing.

Exercise Conventions

The majority of interbank currency options are European exercise convention, meaning that they can be exercised only on the last day of their life. Strictly speaking, the holder of an option has a 24-hour window in which to exercise a European option.

A smaller number of interbank currency options are American exercise, which means they can be exercised at any time in their life.

The most popular option expiration cutoff time is 10:00 A.M. New York time (called the *New York cut*). Some options expire at 3 P.M. Tokyo time (*Tokyo cut*).

Exercise Mechanics

Upon exercise, a currency option turns into a spot foreign exchange deal done at the option strike for settlement on the spot value date. For example, suppose that the holder of the yen call in Exhibit 3.1 elected to exercise on the expiration date, which happened to be a Monday. Barring bank holidays, the exercise would obligate the holder of the option to deliver $10,000,000 to the option writer's account in a New York bank and obligate the option writer to deliver 1,145,800,000 yen to the option holder's account in a Tokyo bank for value on Wednesday.

The holder of the yen put displayed in Exhibit 3.1 would be rational to exercise the option at expiration if the spot exchange rate exceeds the option strike of 114.58. Suppose that the spot exchange rate on exercise day is equal to 115.00. Exercise would mean that the option holder would receive delivery of the dollar face amount, equal to $10,000,000, and would be obligated to make delivery of the yen face amount, equal to 1,145,800,000.

The exercise of the option leaves the option holder with a position that is long dollars and short yen. Normally, the exerciser of an option seeks to realize value by doing a spot transaction to liquidate the cash flow consequences of the exercise. For example, the exerciser of the yen put could sell dollars and buy exactly 1,145,800,000 yen. The residual sum of dollars would be equal to $36,521.74:

$$\$10,000,000 - \frac{1,145,800,000 \ yen}{115.00} = \$36,521.74$$

Alternatively, the option holder could sell exactly 10,000,000 dollars against yen. This would leave a net amount of 4,200,000 yen:

$$\$10,000,000 \times 115.00 - 1,145,800,000 = 4,200,000 \ yen$$

At-the-Money-Forward Options

Currency options that are struck at the prevailing forward exchange rate at the time they are dealt are called *at-the-money-forward* (ATMF) options. This is the case for the call and put in Exhibit 3.1.

An ATMF *straddle* is the combination of an ATMF put and an ATMF call. ATMF currency straddles comprise a large portion of all option trading between option dealers. Their properties are discussed in Chapter 5.

Option Prices

Currency option dealers quote prices to customers in a variety of equivalent ways. Options can be quoted either in currency or as a percentage of face value. The USD put/JPY call[1] in Exhibit 3.1 is quoted as .00020195 dollars per unit of yen face. To arrive at the exact number of dollars, multiply the dollars per unit of yen face times the yen face amount:

$$0.00020195 \left(\frac{USD}{JPY}\right) \times 1,145,800,000\ JPY = \$231,394$$

Alternatively, the quote in yen per unit of dollar face, 2.6611, can be multiplied by the dollar face amount to arrive at the price of the option in yen:

$$2.6611 \left(\frac{JPY}{USD}\right) \times \$10,000,000 = 26,611,000\ JPY$$

The second method, using yen per unit of dollar face, is more familiar because 2.6611 corresponds to the usual way that dollar/yen is quoted. In the language of the spot dealers, the option costs approximately 266 yen pips.

A third method, and the simplest way to quote the option, is as a percentage of face value. The USD call/JPY put in Exhibit 3.1 is quoted as 2.31 percent of face, as can easily be calculated:

$$\frac{\$231,394}{\$10,000,000} = 2.31\%$$

A Sample Interbank Confirmation

Exhibit 3.2 displays a sample interbank option confirmation that can be regarded as industry standard in several important respects:

---

1. When calculated to a sufficient number of decimal digits, the premiums on the yen call and yen put in Exhibit 3.1 are slightly different in value, yet they are both struck at-the-money-forward (ATMF). This would seem to contradict a well-known theorem that the value of an ATMF call must be equal to that of an ATMF put (Chapter 4). The reason for the discrepancy is that the strike price, which is calculated from the interest parity theorem, is rounded to two decimal digits, following the convention of the interbank market to quote dollar/yen to a precision of two pips.

EpiCenter Bank, Inc.
San Francisco, CA

June 21, 1999

Ballistic Trading Partners
Greenwich, CT

Gentlemen:

For a premium of 26,611,000 yen, receipt of which is due on June 23, 1999, you may call on the undersigned for up to 1,145,800,000 yen, at a USD per JPY rate of 114.58. You may exercise this European Style option up to 10:00 AM New York time only on July 21, 1999 (the "Expiration Date") by telephone notice to the undersigned, confirmed in writing, indicating the amount of the currency you have elected to purchase, whereupon delivery and settlement shall be made on July 23, 1999. If the Expiration Date is not a New York business day, the Expiration Date shall be the next succeeding business day.

This option may not be assigned by either party and any such assignment shall be void and of no force or effect.

Unless you instruct us otherwise by 10:00 AM New York time on the Expiration Date, this option shall be deemed to be automatically exercised if at such time on such date it is in-the-money.

Acceptance by you of the premium constitutes your representation that you have substantial assets and/or liabilities denominated in the currency underlying this option, are in the business of trading or investing in such currency, in options in such currency or in assets and/or liabilities denominated in such currency or are otherwise a commercial user of such currency, and that you will be entering into such transaction for purposes related to your business in such currency.

The parties hereby consent to the jurisdiction of a state or federal court situation in New York City, New York in connection with any dispute arising hereunder. This option shall be governed and construed in accordance with the laws of the State of New York with regard to the principles of conflict of laws.

Very truly yours,

EpiCenter Bank, Inc.

Exhibit 3.2 Sample option confirmation.

The option premium is due two days after trade date and is payable in yen.

Notice of exercise on expiration day must be given before 10:00 A.M. New York time.

The option will be automatically exercised if it is in-the-money at expiration (note well that this may not be true for every dealer!).

The option cannot be assigned to third parties.

There is a certain conformity in interbank option confirmations, as there is in the nomenclature of dealing. Yet confirmations are legally binding contracts and as such must be carefully examined.

Margin Practices for Interbank Currency Options

In most cases, customers who trade interbank currency options are required to have a preexisting spot dealing facility with their dealing bank. This is because exercise of an option creates a spotlike transaction at expiration. Also, this rule can be seen as being part of the effort by a bank to screen for client suitability for option trading. Spot dealing lines are granted only to creditworthy and sophisticated institutions.

In some instances, interbank option dealers permit clients without spot dealing facilities to purchase nondeliverable options. A nondeliverable option pays an option holder the value of any in-the-money exercise at expiration without invoking the physical exchange of currencies. This is similar in concept to the nondeliverable forward transaction described in the previous chapter.

Purchasers of interbank currency options must pay for their option in full two days after the option trade date.

Some dealers credit their customers' trading lines for holding options that are seriously in-the-money in a practice called *delta release*.

Short-sellers of interbank currency options must make margin arrangements with their dealer. The actual terms will depend on the nature of the relationship with the short-seller's bank, but in most instances, the option short-seller is required to post an initial bond and agree to top up the collateral if the option appreciates in value.

Listed Options on Actual Foreign Currency

The Philadelphia Stock Exchange (PHLX) lists options on actual sums of foreign currencies. The Options Clearing Corporation (OCC) is the counterparty to every option buyer and seller. The U.S. Securities and Exchange Commission regulates trading in PHLX options.

Contract Specifications

Contract specifications for currency options listed on the Philadelphia Stock Exchange are displayed in Exhibit 3.3. Most of the options are calls and puts on currency against the U.S. dollar, but a few cross-rate options are listed. PHLX trading is concentrated in American exercise options, but European exercise options are also listed.

Quotation Conventions

PHLX options that are dollar-based are quoted in cents that are multiplied by the deliverable number of units of foreign currency. A PHLX option on the euro (face 62,500 euros) quoted as 2.00 would cost

$$\$.0200 \times 62{,}500 \, EUR = \$1{,}250$$

Options on the Japanese yen are quoted in units equal to 1/100 of one U.S. cent. A PHLX yen option (face 6,250,000 yen) quoted as 0.27 would cost

$$\frac{1}{100} \times \$.0027 \times 6{,}250{,}000 \, JPY = \$168.75$$

PHLX cross-rate options on euro/JPY and euro/GBP are quoted in yen and pounds, respectively. A euro/JPY cross option (face 62,500 euros) quoted as 1.25 would cost

$$1.25 \times 62{,}500 \, EUR = 78{,}125 \, JPY$$

Currency	Size	Premium quotations	Minimum premium change	Strike intervals[a]
Dollar-based				
Australian dollar	50,000 AUD	Cents per unit	$.(00)01 = $5.00	1 cent
British pound	31,250 GBP	Cents per unit	$.(00)01 = $3.1215	1 cent
Canadian dollar	50,000 CAD	Cents per unit	$.(00)01 = $5.00	.5 cent
Euro	62,500 EUR	Cents per unit	$.(00)01 = $6.25	2 cents
Japanese yen	6,250,000 JPY	Hundredths of a cent per unit	$.(0000)01 = $6.25	.005 cent
Swiss franc	62,500 CHF	Cents per unit	$.(00)01 = $6.25	.5 cent
Cross rates				
Euro/British pound[b]	31,250 GBP	GBP per EUR	.(00)01EUR = 3.125 GBP	.0050 EUR
Japanese yen/Euro[b]	62,500 EUR	JPY per EUR	.01 JPY = 625 JPY	.5 JPY

Source: Philadelphia Stock Exchange

Note: The PHLX may continue to offer standardized options contracts on USD/DEM, USD/FRF, GBP/DEM, and DEM/JPY.

[a] Applicable for the nearest three months.

[b] Pending SEC approval.

Exhibit 3.3 The Philadelphia Stock Exchange currency options—standardized currency options contract specifications.

Strike Intervals

PHLX options have standardized strike prices (Exhibit 3.3), as is the case with options on shares of stock, equity indexes, bonds, and currency.

Expiration

The PHLX offers a number of expiration cycles for its physically settled currency options contracts, including midmonth, end-month, and long-term expirations. Expiration, which always coincides with the last day of trading, occurs on quarterly and consecutive monthly cycles—that is, currency options are available for trading with fixed quarterly months of March, June, September, and December and two additional near-term months. Month-end expirations are available in the three nearest months. Expirations for June (18 months) and December (24 months) for the following year are also available for some currencies.

Physically settled currency options expire and cease trading either on the Friday preceding the Wednesday of the expiration month for midmonth and long-term options, or, in the case of month-end currency options, on the last Friday of the expiration month. Standardized options expire at 11:59 P.M. eastern time on expiration day.

Exercise

PHLX currency option exercise requires that notice be given to brokers no later than an established cutoff time during a trading day. The broker in turn gives the exercise order to the OCC. Each day, the OCC randomly assigns exercise notices to the accounts of clearing firms that have open short positions in the option contracts that have been exercised. The clearing firms themselves must then decide which of their customers are to be assigned exercise notices. Exchange regulations require clearing firms to make assignment in one of two ways: either based on random selection or on a first-in, first-out basis.

Exercise settlement normally occurs four business days following the issuance of instructions. The OCC maintains correspondent bank accounts outside of the United States for receipt and delivery of foreign currencies to facilitate option exercise.

Trading Hours

The PHLX currency options market is open from 2:30 A.M. to 2:30 P.M., eastern time, Monday through Friday (except for standardized Canadian dollar options, which trade from 7:00 A.M. to 2:30 P.M., eastern time).

Position Limits

The PHLX establishes a position limit on the maximum number of contracts in an underlying currency that can be controlled by a single entity or individual. Currently, position limits are set at 200,000 contracts on each side of the market (long calls and short puts or short calls and long puts) for standard options. Position limits of 100,000 contracts are set for customized options for Italian lira, Spanish peseta, and Mexican peso only. Options involving the U.S. dollar against other currencies are aggregated for purposes of computing position limits.

Special PHLX Options

The PHLX allows for trading in customized option contracts based on selected currencies. Custom expiration can be established for any business day up to two years from the trade date. Customized options expire at 10:15 A.M., eastern time. The strike price of a customized option may be expressed in any increment out to four decimal digits. Customized options are European exercise only.

The Currency Futures and Futures Options Market

A currency futures option delivers a long or a short position in a currency futures contract upon exercise.

Currency Futures

Currency futures are listed on the Chicago Mercantile Exchange's International Monetary Market, known as CME (IMM), and on several other exchanges around the world.[2] As measured by trad-

---

2. Currency futures contracts are also listed on the New York Board of Trade (formerly FINEX [a division of the New York Cotton Exchange]), the Tokyo Inter-

ing volume, the CME (IMM) is the most important currency futures exchange. This book conducts the discussion of currency and currency futures options in the framework of the CME (IMM) derivatives.

CME (IMM) currency futures are traded in pits in an open outcry environment similar to futures contracts on agricultural and other financial commodities, and on the GLOBEX®$_2$ computerized trading system when the open outcry pits are closed. Also, in October 1999 the CME introduced trading in small-sized currency futures traded around the clock on GLOBEX®$_2$.

The Clearing House of the CME clears all trades in the exchange's listed currency futures and futures options. The CME Clearing House interposes itself between each buyer and seller of every currency futures contract to act as a guarantor of contract performance. This practice allows traders to operate on a net basis regardless of whether their long and short positions might have been initiated against different counterparties. Trading in U.S. currency futures and futures options is regulated by the Commodities Futures Trading Commission.

Contract Specifications

Listed futures contracts have fixed specifications with respect to expiration date, size, and futures tick value (Exhibit 3.4). For example, the CME yen futures contract has a notional value of 12,500,000 yen.

Expiration

The last day of trading in CME (IMM) currency contracts is the second business day immediately preceding the third Wednesday of the contract month. The last day for Canadian dollar futures is the business day preceding the third Wednesday of the contract month. The last day for Brazilian real futures is the last business day of the

---

national Financial Futures Exchange, São Paulo's Bolsa de Mercadorias & Futuros, the Philadelphia Board of Trade, the Amsterdam Exchange (formerly the European Option Exchange), and the MidAmerica Commodity Exchange, the Budapest Commodity Exchange, the Budapest Stock Exchange, the Helsinki Exchanges (formerly the Finnish Options Market Exchange), the Singapore International Monetary Exchange (SIMEX), and the Hong Kong Futures Exchange.

Currency	Size	Futures tick value	Exchange symbol	Option strike intervals	Examples of strike intervals	Expanding daily price limit increment multiples
Australian dollar	100,000 AUD	$10.00	AD	$0.01	$0.76 and $0.77	$0.0400
Brazilian real	100,000 BR	$10.00	BR	$0.01	$1.06000 and $1.0700	$0.0600[b]
British pound[a]	62,500 BP	$12.50	BP	$0.02	$1.440 and $1.4600	$0.0800
Canadian dollar	100,000 CAD	$10.00	CD	$0.005	$0.800 and $0.805	$0.0400
Deutsche mark	125,000 DEM	$12.50	DM	$0.01	$0.63 and $0.64	$0.0400[c]
Euro	125,000 EUR	$12.50	EC	$0.01	$1.0500 and $1.0600	$0.0800
French franc	500,000 FRF	$10.00	FR	$0.0025	$0.18000 and $0.18250	$0.01000
Japanese yen	12,500,000 JPY	$12.50	JY	$0.0001	$0.0072 and $0.0073	$0.000400
Mexican peso	500,000 MXP	$12.50	MP	$0.0025	$0.09750 and $0.1000	$0.02000
New Zealand dollar	100,000 NZD	$10.00	NE	$0.01	$0.70 and $0.71	$0.0500
Russian ruble	500,000 RUB	$12.50	RU	$0.005	$0.04000 and $0.04500	$0.02000
S. African rand	500,000 SAR	$12.50	RA	$0.0050	$0.2150 and $0.2200	$0.01000
Swiss franc	125,000 CHF	$12.50	SF	$0.01	$0.72 and $0.73	$0.0400

[a]The minimum fluctuation in the British pound futures is 2 ticks.

[b]Expanding daily price limit applies only to the third and deferred contract months. The first and second Brazilian real futures contract months trade without price limits. The price limit multiple is subject to change depending on the settlement price levels of the underlying futures contract on the last business day of the prior month.

[c]The Deutsche mark futures expanding price limit applied only to pit trading. At the present time, the Deutsche mark futures trade exclusively on GLOBEX®₂ so the price limit is irrelevant.

Exhibit 3.4 Listed currency futures and futures options—Chicago Mercantile Exchange.

contract month for the Central Bank of Brazil. The last trading day for Russian ruble futures in the 15th calendar day of the contract month.

Quotation Conventions

The CME (IMM) quotes futures American quotation style. Exhibit 3.4 displays the value of one futures tick for each contract.

Margin (Performance Bond) Requirements

The Clearing House of the CME sets minimum initial and maintenance margin, or performance bond, rules for trading in currency futures. The exchange rules differentiate speculators from hedgers. The CME (IMM) has special margin rules for intracurrency spreads, such as long one March, short one June Swiss franc futures. Intercurrency spreads, such as a position that is long Australian dollar futures and simultaneously short Canadian dollar futures, also have exceptions. Initial margin can be met with cash or U.S. Treasury securities, but in the case of the latter, a haircut is applied, meaning that the security will count as something less than 100 cents on the dollar.

Daily variation margin operates to pay and collect the gains and losses on futures every day. Variation margin is based on successive changes in the daily settlement price. In theory, the settlement price will be the last bona fide price at the close of a trading session. However, in practice, determination of a fair settlement price can be difficult because of the nature of the open outcry system, where many trades can occur simultaneously at the close. In these cases, the settlement price can be the average of the highest and lowest trades that are done at the close. When no trade is done at the close, the Clearing House is permitted to use special procedures that take into account the historical relationship between contract months. The procedures that govern settlement prices are specified in Exchange Rule 813.

Long positions in futures contracts receive positive variation margin and pay negative variation margin. Short futures positions do just the opposite; they pay positive variation margin and receive negative variation margin.

On the day that a position is opened, variation margin is based on the difference between the traded price and the settlement price that day. Thereafter, the daily variation margin is based on the difference between the settlement price that day and the settlement price on the previous day. On the day when the position is closed, the variation is based on the difference between the traded price and the previous day's settlement price.

Trading Hours

CME regular trading hours are 7:20 A.M. to 2:00 P.M. central standard time. This applies to the currency futures and currency futures options. Trading is also done on the electronic medium GLOBEX2 from 2:30 P.M. to 7:05 A.M. Monday to Thursday and also at selected times on Sundays and holidays.

Price Fluctuation Limits

At present, the CME (IMM) has no price limits for the first 15 minutes of trading during regular trading hours. A schedule of sequential expanding daily price limits becomes effective after the opening 15-minute interval ends. The current expanding price limit increments are displayed in Exhibit 3.4. In the event that the primary futures contract is limit bid or limit offered at an expanding price limit, that expanding price limit goes into effect for a 5-minute period. At the end of the 5-minute period, a new expanding price limit, which is a multiple of the previous limit, comes into effect.

Position Limits

The IMM enforces limits on the size of the position that any one investor may accumulate in a single currency. The limit combines the investor's position in both IMM futures and futures options. Futures options are counted on a delta-adjusted basis. The delta of an option is the dollar amount by which its price ought to change when the price of the underlying asset changes by one unit. The concept of delta will be covered in later chapters. But for now, if the delta of a call option is .5, the CME market surveillance department counts the option as .5 futures contracts in the calculation of an investor's position limit.

Speculative limits on certain currencies are subject to the CME position accountability rule that was approved by the Commodities Futures Trading Commission on January 2, 1992. Under this rule, any market participant who holds or controls a position in

Euro, German mark, Japanese yen, British pound, or Swiss franc futures and futures options contracts that exceed 10,000 contracts net long or short across combined contract months "shall provide, in a timely fashion, upon request by the Exchange, information regarding the nature of the position, trading strategy, and hedging information if applicable."

Exchange for Physical Transactions

Currency futures and spot foreign exchange are linked through a specialized trading market in *exchange for physical* (EFP) transactions. In an EFP trade, a long or short position in a currency futures contract is exchanged for an equivalent face position in spot foreign exchange. EFP trades are referred to as *ex-pit transactions* because they are executed at off-market prices. EFPs are quoted as two-way prices for either buying futures/selling spot or selling futures/buying spot. In normal markets, the EFP market closely follows the level of the swap points in the forward market for value on futures expiration.

One important function of the EFP market is to allow currency futures traders to unwind cash market stop-loss orders or limit orders that were executed outside of floor trading hours. The purpose of an EFP trade is to swap the futures and cash positions to flatten both positions.

The Concept of Basis

The difference between the futures price and the spot exchange rate is called the basis. The basis in currency futures is analogous to the forward points in a currency forward transaction. In theory, the basis is a function of the time to expiration, the level of the spot rate, and the spread between the interest rates of the currencies in question. The term *calendar basis* means the spread in prices between two futures contracts on the same currency but with different expiration dates.

Currency Futures Options

Contract Specifications

The Index and Options Market of the Chicago Mercantile Exchange, referred to as CME (IOM), lists American-style put and call options on their currency futures contracts (Exhibit 3.4). Trading on the IOM is regulated by the Commodities Futures Trading Commission.

Quotation Conventions

The rule for quoting futures options is similar to the procedures of the Philadelphia exchange for currency options. Quotations for futures options are given in U.S. cents, which are multiplied by the deliverable futures contract's quantity of foreign currency. A futures option on the euro quoted at $0.0124 would be worth

$$\$0.0124 \times 125,000\ EUR = \$1,550.00$$

One exception to the rule is the Japanese yen futures option, which is quoted in cents per 100 yen.

Expiration

The CME (IOM) lists currency futures options for quarterly expiration (that follow the March quarterly cycle), for monthly expiration for serial months (i.e., months that are not in the March quarterly cycle), and for weekly expiration. Quarterly and monthly expiration options cease trading on the second Friday immediately preceding the third Wednesday of the contract month (with special rules for options on futures on the Brazilian real and South African rand).

Margin (Performance Bond) Rules for Futures Options

The CME (IOM) determines futures option margin, or performance bond, requirements using a proprietary software program that it calls SPAN (Standard Portfolio Analysis of Risk). SPAN sets margin requirements according to estimates of the maximum one-day loss that a position might suffer. SPAN generates daily margin requirements based on portfolio risk analysis and scenario models of changing market conditions. SPAN arrays are provided daily to clearing firms to calculate minimum margin requirements.

Exercise of CME (IOM) Futures Options

CME (IOM) futures options may be exercised on any business day that the option is traded. To exercise an option, the clearing member representing the buyer must present an exercise notice to the Clearing House by 7:00 P.M. of the day of exercise.

Exercise notices that are accepted by the Clearing House are assigned by a process of random selection to clearing members that have open short option positions. Clearing firms then assign exercise to one or more of their clients who have short positions in the particular futures option that has been exercised.

The deliverable asset underlying a currency futures option is a currency futures contract. Following exercise, the delivered futures position becomes a live position on the trading day immediately following the exercise. Exercise creates long and short futures contract positions in the accounts of the option owner and writer, according to the following rule:

Exercise of a Futures Option

	Call option	Put option
Owner of the option	Long future	Short future
Writer of the option	Short future	Long future

The deliverable futures contract is the one that is next after expiration in the March-June-September-December cycle. The exercise of an October futures options would result in the delivery of a December futures contract. The spread between the option strike and the futures settlement price is thereupon reflected in the accounts of the clearing firms and in their clients' accounts. If on a day in May, the owner of a June Deutsche mark call struck at 575 were to exercise, he would be credited with a long June futures position and a mark-to-market equal to

$$(.5875 - .5750) \times 125{,}000 = \$1{,}562.50$$

where .5875 is the settlement price of the June futures contract on that day. Initial and variation margin rules for the futures contract immediately come into force.

Position Limits and Price Fluctuation Constraints

The CME enforces position limits on the combined number of futures and futures options contacts on a single currency that an investor may hold or control. The market surveillance department counts futures options on a delta-adjusted basis.

The CME sets price fluctuation limits on currency futures during the first 15 minutes of every trading session. Throughout the day, futures options trading automatically halts whenever the underlying futures contract locks-limit.

Chapter **4**

European Currency Options

A European currency option is a put or a call on a sum of foreign currency that can be exercised only on the final day of its life. This chapter discusses the valuation of European currency options. The chapter begins with various arbitrage and parity theorems and then advances to the important Black-Scholes model for European currency options as adapted by Garman and Kohlhagen (1983).

The following conventions will be used throughout this book:

C is the value of a European currency call option

P is the value of a European currency put option

S is the spot exchange rate

K is the option strike

R_f is the interest rate on the foreign currency

R_d is the interest rate on the domestic currency

For the purpose of presenting theoretical material, it will be assumed that the deliverable underlying asset of a basic put and call is one unit of foreign exchange. Both S and K are denominated in units of domestic currency (i.e., expressed in American spot convention). One unit of foreign currency is worth S units of domestic currency.

In this framework, a call is the right but not the obligation to surrender K units of domestic currency to receive one unit of foreign currency. A put is the right but not the obligation to surrender one unit of foreign currency and receive K units of domestic currency.

The current time is denoted as t. Option expiration occurs at time T. The remaining time to expiration is τ, which by definition is equal to $T - t$.

Arbitrage Theorems

Arbitrage is defined as the simultaneous purchase and sale of two securities or combinations of securities in an attempt to earn a riskless profit.

Arbitrage opportunities do exist in the market on occasion but usually only for brief periods. When they are discovered, traders with ready sources of capital are quick to take advantage. Whatever is cheap soon becomes more expensive and whatever is expensive soon becomes cheaper. The process stops only when such opportunities are "arbitraged out" of the market. In equilibrium, no permanent arbitrage opportunities should exist; this is referred to as the *no-arbitrage condition* or the *no-arbitrage rule*. A central tenet of capital markets theory is that all assets, including foreign exchange and options on foreign exchange, should be priced in the market consistent with the no-arbitrage rule.

Four elementary theorems of currency option pricing follow from the no-arbitrage rule (see Gibson 1991 and Grabbe 1996):

Option Values at Expiration

The value of a call and a put at expiration is given by

$$C_T = Max[0, S_T - K]$$
$$P_T = Max[0, K - S_T]$$

where C_T, P_T, and S_T are the values of the call, the put, and the spot exchange rate at expiration time T, respectively.

Options Have Nonnegative Prices

The price of an option cannot be less than zero. That is,

$$C \geq 0, \quad P \geq 0$$

The rationale is that because an option confers the right but not the obligation to exercise, it can never have a negative value.

Upper Boundaries for Options

The maximum value for a European call is the spot value of the underlying deliverable currency:

$$C \leq S$$

If this were not true, an arbitrage profit would exist from selling the option and buying the deliverable underlying foreign currency, the latter having value equal to S. Likewise, the maximum value for a European put is the value of the deliverable domestic currency, which has value equal to the strike:

$$P \leq K$$

Lower Boundaries for European Options

The greater lower boundaries for currency calls and puts are given by

$$C \geq e^{-R_f \tau} S - e^{R_d \tau} K$$

$$P \geq e^{-R_d \tau} K - e^{-R_f \tau} S$$

The terms $e^{-R_f \tau}$ and $e^{-R_d \tau}$ represent the continuous-time present value operators for the foreign and domestic interest rates, respectively.

To verify the inequality for the call, consider the following transaction involving two portfolios. The first portfolio consists of a long position in a call plus a long position in a domestic currency zero coupon bond that pays the deliverable amount of domestic currency, equal to the strike, at expiration (its present value is equal to $e^{-R_d \tau} K$); the second portfolio consists of a zero coupon foreign currency bond that pays one unit of foreign currency at the option's expiration date (its present value would be equal to $e^{-R_f \tau} S$). The payoff matrix at expiration would be

	$S_T \leq K$	$S_T > K$
Portfolio 1		
Long call	0	$S_T - K$
Long domestic bond	K	K
Total value	K	S_T
Portfolio 2		
Long foreign bond	S_T	S_T
Total value	S_T	S_T

Taking a long position in portfolio 1 and a short position in portfolio 2 would create a nonnegative payoff at expiration

	$S_T \leq K$	$S_T > K$
Portfolio 1 – Portfolio 2	$K - S_T \geq 0$	0

Because the expiration value of the first portfolio is greater than or equal to that of the second portfolio, the no-arbitrage rule forces the value of the first portfolio to be greater than or equal to the value of the second portfolio before expiration:

$$C + e^{-R_d \tau} K \geq e^{-R_f \tau} S_t$$

which completes the proof. A similar proof can be constructed for European puts.

Put-Call Parity for European Currency Options

Put-call parity is an arbitrage linkage between the prices of put and call options. It states that at any time before expiration, the difference between the price of a European put and a European call having the same strike and same expiration must be equal to the difference between (a) the present value of the deliverable quantity of domestic currency (i.e., the strike) and (b) the present value of the deliverable quantity of foreign currency.

The trick to understanding put-call parity is to realize that if you were long a put and short a call, you would in effect have a short position in the foreign currency and a long position in the domestic currency, regardless of the level of the exchange rate on expiration day. This is because if the put finishes in-the-money, you would exercise, meaning you would deliver foreign currency and receive domestic currency. But the same thing would happen if the short call finishes in-the-money. The call would be exercised against you, and again you would be obligated to deliver foreign exchange and receive domestic. If both options finish at-the-money, both would be worthless, but on the other hand, the deliverable quantity of foreign exchange would exactly equal the value of the deliverable quantity of domestic currency.

More formally, European put-call parity can be demonstrated by considering two portfolios. Portfolio 1 consists of a long European put and short European call having the same strike and expiration. At expiration, the deliverable quantity of foreign currency upon exercise of either option is one unit, which will be worth S_T. Portfolio 2 consists of a long position in a zero coupon bond that pays the deliverable quantity of domestic currency upon exercise, which will be worth K, plus a short position in a foreign currency zero coupon bond that pays one unit of foreign exchange at expiration. The equivalence of portfolio 1 and portfolio 2 can be demonstrated with the following expiration-day payoff matrix.

	$S_T \leq K$	$S_T > K$
Portfolio 1		
Long put	$K - S_T$	0
Short call	0	$-(S_T - K)$
Total value	$K - S_T$	$K - S_T$
Portfolio 2		
Long domestic bond	K	K
Short foreign bond	$-S_T$	$-S_T$
Total value	$K - S_T$	$K - S_T$

Because at expiration the two payoff matrices are equal, the cost of creating the portfolios before expiration must be equal. The cost of portfolio 1 is the difference between the put and the call. The cost of portfolio 2 is the difference between the present values of the domestic bond that pays the strike at expiration and the foreign currency bond that pays one unit of foreign exchange at expiration. This completes the demonstration of put-call parity, which can be expressed algebraically as

$$P - C = e^{-R_d \tau} K - e^{-R_f \tau} S$$

One immediate implication of put-call parity is that the value of at-the-money-forward European puts and calls that have a common expiration must be equal. This can be seen by substituting the value of the interest parity forward rate for the strike K in the put-call parity formula:

$$K = F = e^{(R_d - R_f)\tau} S$$

then

$$P - C = e^{-R_d \tau} e^{(R_d - R_f)\tau} S - e^{-R_f \tau} S = 0$$

Option traders have developed a convenient paradigm for decomposing the value of an in-the-money (relative to the forward) currency option using put-call parity. Consider a call that is in-the-money, meaning that the prevailing forward outright exceeds the option strike ($F > K$). According to put-call parity, that option is worth

$$C = P + e^{-R_f \tau} S - e^{-R_d \tau} K$$

which can be written as

$$C = P + e^{-R_d \tau}(F - K)$$

If C is in-the-money-forward, then it follows that a same-strike put, P, is out-of-the-money-forward. The value of such a put is pure optionality, so to speak, or what traders call *volatility value*. Traders call the absolute value of the expression $(F - K)$ *parity to forward*. The term $e^{-R_d \tau}$ is a present value operator. All together, the value of the call is the sum of its volatility value and the present value of its parity to forward.

The Black-Scholes-Merton Model

The European option model was developed in stages by several theoreticians. The genesis for the idea comes from the well-known Black-Scholes (1973) model that was developed for a European call option on shares of a common stock that does not pay dividends. Merton (1973) extended this model to the theoretical case of an option on shares of a stock that pays dividends continuously. Finally, Garman and Kohlhagen (1983) adapted the model to work for European options on foreign currencies. We will refer to this as the *Black-Scholes-Merton* or BSM model.[1]

Three Assumptions

Like all theoretical models, BSM requires some simplifying assumptions:

1. There are no taxes, no transactions costs, and no restrictions on taking long or short positions in options and currency. All transactors are price takers. This means that no single economic agent can buy or sell in sufficient size so as to control market prices.

2. The foreign and domestic interest rates are riskless and constant over the term of the option's life. All interest rates are expressed as continuously compounded rates.

3. Instantaneous changes in the spot exchange rate are generated by a *diffusion process* (sometimes called an *Ito process* or *geometric Brownian motion*) of the form

$$\frac{dS}{S} = \mu dt + \sigma dz$$

---

1. The option-pricing model for currency options is called by a variety of different names, ranging from Black-Scholes to Black-Scholes-Garman-Kohlhagen to Garman-Kohlhagen. Yet with no disrespect to Garman and Kohlhagen's work, it is clear that the critical thought process originated from Black, Scholes, and Merton. Black's "How We Came Up with the Option Formula" (1989) gives an interesting account of the discovery of the model and discusses Merton's contribution. Emanuel Derman's 1996 article "Reflections on Fischer" has further insights into Black's thinking on how the model came into existence.

where μ is the instantaneous drift and dt is an instant in time. Said another way, the term μ represents the risk premium on the spot exchange rate, σ is the instantaneous standard deviation, and dz is the differential of a stochastic variable; dz is normally distributed with mean zero and standard deviation equal to the square root of dt.

The first assumption is a standard one that appears in many financial models, sometimes called the *frictionless markets condition*. The second assumption is the key modification to the Black-Scholes model to make it work for options on foreign exchange. The interest rate on the foreign currency plays a role analogous to that of the continuous dividend in the Merton version of the model for common stocks. The third assumption specifies that the stochastic process that generates exchange rates is a diffusion process. This particular process implies that the spot exchange rate level, S_t, is distributed lognormal and that the natural log return series

$$\ln \frac{S_t}{S_{t-1}}$$

is normally distributed with mean

$$\left(\mu - \frac{\sigma^2}{2} \right)$$

and standard deviation σ (see Hull 1997).

Six parameters must be known to use the BSM model:

S: The spot exchange rate quoted in units of domestic currency

K: The strike quoted in units of domestic currency

τ: The time remaining to expiration measured in years

R_f: The foreign currency interest rate

R_d: The domestic currency interest rate

σ: The annualized standard deviation of the spot exchange rate

The Local Hedge Concept

The heart of the BSM model is the idea that it is theoretically possible to operate a dynamic local hedge for a currency option using long or short positions in foreign exchange. The local hedge must be rebalanced in response to infinitesimally small changes in exchange rates. Consider the following example of the yen call described in the previous chapter:

USD Put/JPY Call

Face in USD	$10,000,000
Face in JPY	1,145,800,000
Strike	114.58
Spot	115.00
Term	30 days
Interest rate (USD)	5.00%
Interest rate (JPY)	0.50%
Volatility	20.25%
Value in USD	$230,827
Exercise convention	European

The price of this option is $230,827 at a dollar/yen spot exchange rate of 115.00. Suppose that in an instant the spot exchange rate rises to 115.20. In fact, if nothing else were to change, the value of this option would fall to $222,080, or by $8,747.

Suppose that before the move in the exchange rate, one hedged a long position in the option with a long position in spot dollar/yen with face equal to $10 million dollar/yen. The idea of hedging using a long position in dollar/yen to hedge a dollar put option may seem counterintuitive at first, but not when it is understood that the value of the option, being a put on the dollar or call on the yen, is bound to fall if dollar/yen rises. The hedge works by making money when dollar/yen rises. If dollar/yen rises by 20 pips, from 115.00 to 115.20, the exact profit on the hedge would be $17,361.

Yet the size of the hedge is clearly too large because the loss in the value of the option is only $8,747. A smaller-sized hedge, say, in the amount of the ratio

$$\frac{8,747}{17,361} = .5038$$

which would be long $5,038,000 USD/JPY, is an almost perfect fit. A spot position of that size would gain $8,746, on the move from 115.00 to 115.20.

The ratio .5038 is a crude estimate for what in option theory is called the delta (δ). Delta is the absolute change in value of the option when the exchange rate changes either up or down by one unit. Delta itself changes when the spot exchange rate changes (and when other variables change as well). Delta is bounded in absolute value by zero and one for European options.

An option that is far-out-of-the-money has a delta near zero because a unit change in the spot exchange rate would not make much of a difference to the option; except for a tremendous change in the spot rate, the option is likely to expire out-of-the-money. At the other extreme, an option that is deep-in-the-money should move up and down in almost equal unit value (delta near to one in absolute value) with the underlying changes in the spot rate. This is because changes in the spot rate are likely captured in the option's value at expiration. An option with delta exactly equal to one in absolute value would move up and down in value in an equivalent way to a spot foreign exchange position with size equal to the option face.

Continuing with the local hedge, if at every point in time it were possible to recalculate delta and accordingly maintain the correct size of the spot hedge, the position in the option would be perfectly protected against movements in the spot exchange rate. As such, the aggregate position in the option and the hedge would be risk-less. According to capital market theory, such a combination must earn no more and no less than the riskless rate of interest. Although the idea of a local hedge seems highly impractical, the mere theoretical possibility that it could be successfully operated is, in fact, a key element in the option-pricing model.

The Model in Terms of Spot Exchange Rates

Under the assumption that it is possible to operate a perfect local hedge between a currency option and underlying foreign exchange,

Garman and Kohlhagen, following Black, Scholes, and Merton, derive the following partial differential equation

$$\frac{1}{2}\sigma^2 S^2 \frac{\partial^2 C}{\partial S^2} - R_d C + (R_d S - R_f S)\frac{\partial C}{\partial S} - \frac{\partial C}{\partial \tau} = 0$$

This equation governs the pricing of a currency call option. When the expiration day payoff function

$$C_T = \text{Max}[0, S_T - K]$$

is imposed as a boundary condition, the partial differential equation can be solved to obtain the BSM value for the call. The derivation of the put follows along the same lines.

The BSM Model

$$C = e^{-R_f \tau} S N(x + \sigma \sqrt{\tau}) - e^{-R_d \tau} K N(x)$$

$$P = e^{-R_f \tau} S\left(N(x + \sigma \sqrt{\tau}) - 1\right) - e^{R_d \tau} K\left(N(x) - 1\right)$$

$$x = \frac{\ln\left(\frac{S}{K}\right) + \left(R_d - R_f - \frac{\sigma^2}{2}\right)\tau}{\sigma \sqrt{\tau}}$$

where C is the premium of a European call
P is the premium of a European put
S is the spot exchange rate (units of domestic currency)
K is the strike (units of domestic currency)
τ is the remaining time to expiration in years
R_f is the foreign currency interest rate
R_d is the domestic interest rate
σ is the standard deviation of the spot exchange rate
$N(\cdot)$ is the cumulative normal density function[2]

---

2. Abramowitz and Stegun's 1972 *Handbook of Mathematical Functions* (paragraph 26.2.17) gives the following polynomial approximation for the cumulative normal density function for variable x:

The first derivative of the theoretical value of these options is the delta mentioned earlier. The call delta is given by

$$\delta_{call} = e^{-R_f \tau} N(x + \sigma\sqrt{\tau})$$

There is extensive discussion of option partial derivatives in the next chapter.

An alternative formulation of the model uses the forward outright to stand in the place of the spot exchange rate. The value date for the forward outright, F, is the option expiration date. The equations for calls and puts are

The BSM Model in Terms of the Forward Exchange Rate

$$C = e^{-R_d \tau}\left[FN(y + \sigma\sqrt{\tau}) - KN(y)\right]$$

$$P = e^{-R_d \tau}\left[F\left(N(y + \sigma\sqrt{\tau}) - 1\right) - K\left(N(y) - 1\right)\right]$$

$$y = \frac{\ln\left(\frac{F}{K}\right) - \left(\frac{\sigma^2}{2}\right)\tau}{\sigma\sqrt{\tau}}$$

where all the variables are as previously defined and the forward outright can be derived from the interest parity formula

$$F = Se^{(R_d - R_f)\tau}$$

—————

$$y = \frac{1}{1 + .2316419x}$$

$$N(x) = 1 - Z(x)(b_1 y + b_2 y^2 + b_3 y^3 + b_4 y^4 + b_5 y^5) + e(x)$$

$$Z(x) = \frac{1}{\sqrt{2\pi}}e^{-\frac{x^2}{2}}$$

where

$b_1 = .319381530$
$b_2 = -0.356563782$
$b_3 = 1.781477937$
$b_4 = -1.821255978$
$b_5 = 1.330274429$

If x is less than zero, $N(x) = 1 - N(x)$. The absolute value of the error term should be less than 7.5×10^{-8}.

The Cox-Ross Risk-Neutral Explanation

Cox and Ross (1976) provide an insight into the unimportance of investor attitudes toward risk in option-pricing theory.

Cox and Ross note that the Black-Scholes partial differential equation contains no variable that is dependent on investor risk preferences (for example, the term μ, which can be thought of as the risk premium for foreign exchange, is not present in the option model). Therefore, an option should be equally valuable to a risk-averse investor and to a risk-neutral investor, provided that it is at least theoretically possible to construct a perfect local hedge.

Consider how a risk-neutral investor would value a call option on foreign currency. At expiration, there can be only two realizations: either the call will be worthless, if it is at-the-money or out-of-the-money, or it will be worth the difference between the exchange rate and the strike. The first case would be ignored by the risk-neutral investor. Only the second case matters. The value of the option is equal to the present value, using the riskless interest rate, of the conditional expectation of the future spot exchange rate minus the strike. The mathematical expectation is conditional on the option being in-the-money at expiration. The probability of the option being in-the-money at expiration and the expected value of the spot exchange rate at expiration can be derived from the cumulative lognormal density function for the spot exchange rate. Following Gemmill (1993) and Jarrow and Rudd (1983), the option model can be decomposed into the following parts:

$$[e^{-R_d\tau}][N(x)]\left[e^{(R_d-R_f)\tau}S\frac{N(x+\sigma\sqrt{\tau})}{N(x)} - K\right]$$

The first term in brackets is the present value factor. The second term[3] is the risk-neutral probability that the option will finish in-the-money. The third term is the expected payoff at expiration conditional on the option finishing in-the-money.

---

3. Among currency traders it is popular to speak of the probability of all kinds of events as *deltas*. If the trader thinks something is likely to occur, she might say, "I am a ninety delta." Something that is unlikely might be a "15 delta." Mathematically, the delta of a BSM call option,

$$e^{-R_f\tau}N(x+\sigma\sqrt{\tau})$$

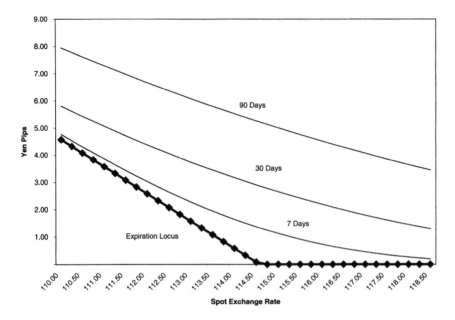

Exhibit 4.1   USD put/JPY call.

The Geometry of the Model

Exhibit 4.1 shows a graph of the USD put/JPY call that has been the running example in this chapter's discussion. The option is displayed at four stages of its life: 90 days, 30 days, 7 days, and expiration. The horizontal axis is the spot exchange rate and the vertical axis is the theoretical value of the option in yen pips. At expiration, the value of the option is given by

$$C_T = Max[0, S_T - K]$$

Graphically, the expiration locus is the familiar option "hockey stick." All three live options lie above the expiration locus.

The slope of the option line with respect to the spot exchange rate is the delta. As time remaining to expiration elapses, meaning that the option ages, the theoretical curve for the call shifts down-

---

is close in value to $N(x)$, provided the foreign currency interest rate is not large. The term $N(x)$ is the risk-neutral probability that the option will finish in-the-money.

ward and to the right—in effect, the curve drops and sags (and therefore becomes convex, which is a topic for the next chapter). Finally, at expiration, the curve collapses on its expiration locus.

A Numerical Example

Consider a numerical example of how to calculate the value of a European currency option using the BSM model:

USD Put/JPY Call

Face in USD	$10,000,000
Face in JPY	1,145,800,000
Strike	114.58
Spot	115.00
Term	30 days
Interest rate (USD)	5.00%
Interest rate (JPY)	0.50%
Volatility	20.25%
Exercise convention	European

The BSM model classifies this option as a call (i.e., a yen call). To calculate the value of the option, first find the value of x:

$$x = \frac{\ln\left(\frac{\frac{1}{115.00}}{\frac{1}{114.58}}\right) + \left(5.00\% - 0.50\% - \frac{(20.25\%)^2}{2}\right)\frac{30}{365}}{20.25\% \times \sqrt{\frac{30}{365}}} = -.0283424$$

and the related expression

$$x + \sigma\sqrt{\tau} = x + 20.25\% \times \sqrt{\frac{30}{365}} = .0297125$$

Next find the cumulative normal densities (see the approximation procedure in footnote 2):

$$N(x) = .4886945$$

$$N(x + \sigma\sqrt{\tau}) = .5118519$$

Next find the value of the option, which in this case is a call option:

$$C = e^{-0.50\% \frac{30}{365}} \left(\frac{1}{115.00} \right) \times (.5118519) - e^{-5.00\% \frac{30}{365}}$$

$$\left(\frac{1}{114.58} \right) \times (.4886945) = .0002015$$

When multiplied by the yen face amount of the option, 1,145,800,000 yields the dollar value of the option, $230,827.[4]

How Currency Options Trade in the Interbank Market

Professional interbank traders have developed a specialized system for quoting currency options that has its roots in option-pricing concepts. Instead of quoting currency options in terms of dollars or other currencies, traders quote in units of volatility. Once quoted volatility is established, dealers work to get an actual money price for the option from the BSM model.

Consider the following example. Suppose that an investor desires to do a transaction in a one-month, at-the-money-forward USD put/JPY call. A check of the market reveals that one-month *yen volatility* (or just *vol*) is being quoted by dealers at 20.25 percent bid, 20.35 percent ask.

To arrive at the money price of the option, the investor can use the BSM formula (Exhibit 4.2). Based on the indicated levels of volatility, the option is bid at $230,827 (where the investor can sell) and ask at $231,966 (where the investor can buy). Note that there are no commissions connected with buying and selling interbank currency options.

Sample volatilities for major currencies (observed in January 1999) are displayed in Exhibit 4.3. Note that there is a term structure for option volatility and that it can vary widely across exchange rates. Japanese yen volatility was unusually well bid when the levels in the exhibit were observed. All of the volatility levels in Exhibit 4.3 correspond to at-the-money-forward options. Out-of-

---

4. This makes no allowance for rounding. If the truncated number .0002015 is used, the dollar price would be $230,878.

	Dealer's bid	Dealer's ask
Currency pair	USD/JPY	USD/JPY
Put/Call	USD put/JPY call	USD put/JPY call
Customer action	Sells	Buys
Dealer action	Buys	Sells
Face USD	$10,000,000	$10,000,000
Face JPY	1,145,800,000	1,145,800,000
Strike	114.58	114.58
Days to expiry	30	30
Market data		
Spot	115.00	115.00
Forward outright	114.58	114.58
Interest rate (USD)	5.000%	5.000%
Interest rate (JPY)	0.500%	0.500%
Quoted volatility	20.25%	20.35%
Option pricing		
USD pips	0.0002015	0.0002024
Total USD	$230,827	$231,966
JPY pips	2.6545	2.6676
Total JPY	26,545,000	26,676,000
Percentage of face amount	2.31%	2.32%
Dealer's hedge		
Delta (times 100)	(49)	(49)
Hedge (spot)	$4,879,475.40	−$4,878,917

Exhibit 4.2 Dealer's bid and ask for USD put/JPY call.

the-money options can trade at higher levels of volatility, a phenomenon that is called the *smile* and is discussed in Chapter 6.

Traders identify options in the first instance by their delta to gauge the extent of their out-of-the-moneyness. As a rough rule of thumb, at-the-money-forward puts and calls have deltas of approx-

Currency	1 week	1 month	1 year
EUR/USD	9.50	9.80	9.60
USD/JPY	23.50	20.30	17.90
EUR/JPY	25.00	22.00	17.90
EUR/CHF	5.00	5.20	5.10
GBP/USD	9.50	9.50	8.80
GBP/EUR	9.10	9.20	7.80
AUD/USD	12.30	12.00	10.50
USD/CAD	8.00	8.10	8.00
USD/CHF	11.10	11.30	10.80

Exhibit 4.3   Sample foreign exchange option quoted volatilities (at-the-money forward).

imately 50. A *25-delta* option is out-of-the-money. A *15-delta* option is even further out-of-the-money.

As a rule, option dealers buy and sell puts and calls only when the options are accompanied by hedging transactions consisting of spot foreign exchange deals. This convention allows the dealer to trade options on a *delta-neutral* basis. The size of the spot hedging transaction can be calculated by multiplying the delta by the face of the option, as can be seen at the bottom of Exhibit 4.2. The delta for the USD put/JPY call is calculated to be −49. The actual number is really 0.49, but traders multiply by 100. From the dealer's perspective, if he buys the option he needs to buy roughly $4.9 million worth of dollar/yen. If he sells the option, he needs to sell the same amount of dollar/yen.

Customers buy and sell options either *live* (i.e., without a hedge) or *hedged*. In the latter case, it is customary for the customer to exchange spot foreign exchange with the dealer. For example, if the customer buys the USD put/JPY call option in Exhibit 4.2, the spot hedge would consist of the customer buying and the dealer selling $4.9 million dollar/yen.

Reflections on the Contribution of Black, Scholes, and Merton

It is no exaggeration to say that the work of Black, Scholes, and Merton fundamentally transformed the currency option market. Of course, Black-Scholes-type models greatly influenced the development of all derivatives markets. But the impact on the currency option market is one of their greatest enduring practical influences.

The basic paradigm of how trading in currency options operates is rife with Black-Scholes concepts. Options are identified in the first instance not by strike but by their delta. Traders might ask for the 50-delta or 15-delta options, for example. Currency option prices are quoted not in currency but in terms of volatility. The genius of quoting option prices in volatility is that price comparison across currencies, strikes, and term to expiration is instantly achieved. After an option is bought or sold, traders turn to the option-pricing model to transform the volatility price into a price in currency (such as dollars and cents).

Perhaps the most revolutionary concept from Black-Scholes-Merton is their framework for risk analysis. Even in markets where mathematicians have produced second- and third-generation option models, the Black-Scholes-Merton vocabulary, including such terms as delta, gamma, theta, vega, and rho, still permeates the language of option modeling.

Chapter 5

European Currency Option Analytics

The previous chapter developed the industry-standard Black-Scholes-Merton (BSM) model for European currency options. Attention now turns to using the model to understand the dynamics of option valuation and the analysis of option risk.

Base-Case Analysis

In the BSM model, five factors contribute to the valuation of a currency option: the spot exchange rate, the market level of option volatility, the foreign interest rate, the domestic interest rate, and the time to expiration. One way to get a fast look at how these factors work is to examine the change in an option's value when each factor by itself is subject to a small change. Exhibit 5.1 does this experiment on the one-month dollar put/yen call from Chapter 4. Under the base-case assumptions, this option is worth $230,827. When the pricing factors change, the dynamics are as follows:

   A one-yen move in the spot exchange up from 115.00 to 116.00 removes $41,399 of value from the option.

   One day of time decay costs the holder of the option $4,472 as the time to expiration shrinks from 30 days to 29 days.

   A 1 percent increase in market option volatility, meaning a rise from 20.25 percent to 21.25 percent, adds $11,386 to the value of the option.

   An increase in the foreign interest rate by 1 percent, from 0.50 percent to 1.50 percent, subtracts $4,165 from the option value.

   An increase in the domestic interest rate by 1 percent, from 5 percent to 6 percent, adds $4,022 to the value of the option.

	Base-case	Spot exchange rate +1 yen	Time −1 day	Volatility +1%	Foreign interest rate +1%	Domestic interest rate +1%
Currency pair	USD/JPY					
Put/Call	USD Put/JPY Call					
Face USD	$10,000,000					
Face JPY	1,145,800,000					
Strike	114.58					
Days to expiry	30		29			
Market data						
Spot	115.00	116.00				
Forward outright	114.58					
Interest rate (USD)	5.000%					6.00%
Interest rate (JPY)	0.500%				1.50%	
Implied volatility	20.25%			21.250%		
Option pricing						
USD pips	0.0002015	0.0001653	0.0001976	0.0002114	0.0001978	0.0002050
Total USD	$230,827	$189,428	$226,355	$254,213	$226,662	$234,849
Change		**−$41,399**	**−$4,472**	**$11,386**	**−$4,165**	**$4,022**
Spot equivalent						
Delta (times 100)	51	45	51	51	51	52
Delta times face	−$5,116,416	−$4,522,841	−$5,105,978	−$5,122,001	−$5,055,816	−$5,172,835

Exhibit 5.1 Option sensitivity to input parameters.

Yet the full picture is more complex to grasp because the sensitivity of the option to each of the pricing factors is dynamic over the course of the option's life and as the spot exchange rates move toward and away from the option's strike. Moreover, the sensitivity of an option to one pricing factor, for example, to the spot exchange rate, is a function of all the other pricing factors, volatility, time, and interest rates.

The "Greeks"

Exact decomposition of how an option changes when pricing factors change requires knowledge of the partial derivatives of the BSM model for both calls and puts. A partial derivative is the change in a function given an infinitesimally small change in one of its input parameters holding all other parameters constant. Market participants have decided to give these derivatives special names, all but one of which are letters from the Greek alphabet.

Delta and Gamma

The most important partial derivative in option analysis is the delta (δ), which is defined as the partial derivative of the option price with respect to the spot exchange rate. Delta was introduced on a heuristic level in Chapter 4. The appendix to this chapter derives delta using elementary calculus. The call and put deltas are given by

Delta

$$\delta_{call} \equiv \frac{\partial C}{\partial S} = e^{-R_f \tau} N(x + \sigma \sqrt{\tau})$$

$$\delta_{put} \equiv \frac{\partial P}{\partial S} = e^{-R_f \tau} \left(N(x + \sigma \sqrt{\tau}) - 1 \right)$$

The deltas of calls and puts are bounded as follows

$$0 \leq \delta_{call} \leq 1$$

$$-1 \leq \delta_{put} \leq 0$$

The delta of the dollar put/yen call in Exhibit 5.1 is equal to $-.5116$. In practice, currency option traders convert delta into units of one or the other face currencies, such as $5.116 million. What the delta tells the trader is that this option will behave approximately like a short spot position in dollar/yen with face equal to $5,116,000 for small movements in the exchange rate.

Exhibit 5.2 shows the delta of the dollar put/yen call against the level of the spot exchange rate for at-the-money-forward options with 30 and 90 days to expiration. The S-shaped appearance is accounted for by the presence of the cumulative normal density function in the equation for delta.

The deltas of calls and puts with the same strike and expiration are related in the following way:

$$\delta_{call} - \delta_{put} = e^{-R_f \tau}$$

which can be obtained by taking the partial derivative of the put-call parity equation with respect to the spot exchange rate.

Delta is so widely used that its own behavior is studied. The partial derivative of an option's delta with respect to the spot exchange rate is called gamma (γ). Equivalently, gamma is the second-

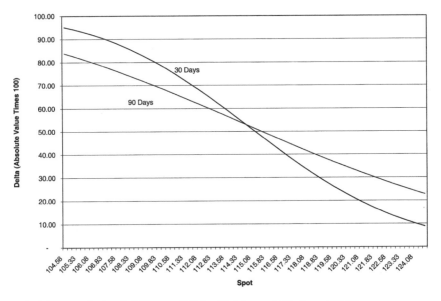

Exhibit 5.2   Delta (USD put/JPY call; 30- and 90-day ATMF; vol = 20.25%; R_d = 5%; R_f = 0.50%).

order partial of the option price with respect to the spot exchange rate. The formula is

Gamma

$$\gamma_{call} = \gamma_{put} = \frac{\partial^2 C}{\partial S^2} = \frac{N'(x + \sigma\sqrt{\tau})e^{-R_f\tau}}{S\sigma\sqrt{\tau}}$$

where N' is the normal density function

$$N'(z) = \frac{1}{\sqrt{2\pi}}e^{\frac{-z^2}{2}}$$

The fact that gamma is equal for calls and puts can be demonstrated by taking the second-order partial of the put-call parity formula with respect to the spot exchange rate.

The gamma for the dollar put/yen call in Exhibit 5.1 is 789.58— this is called *raw gamma* because it needs to be transformed into units that are meaningful. The better way to represent gamma is in terms of the movement in delta for a one-big figure (in this case one yen) movement in the spot exchange rate:

$$\gamma_{1\ big\ figure} = Face \times \left(\frac{1}{S_2} - \frac{1}{S_1}\right) \times \gamma$$

$$\gamma_{1\ big\ figure} = \$10mm \times \left(\frac{1}{116.00} - \frac{1}{115.00}\right) \times 789.58 = -\$591,889$$

This indicates that delta will drop by approximately $600,000 from its base level of $5,116,000 if the spot exchange rate rises to 116.00 from 115.00.

In Exhibit 5.3a, the option with the maximum gamma is nearly at-the-money-forward. In Exhibit 5.3b, options with little time remaining to expiration are very rich in gamma. This is evident by comparing the two S-shaped delta curves in Exhibit 5.2. The 30-day option's delta curve has more curvature, or convexity, than does the 90-day option's delta.

Gamma is analogous to convexity in bonds. For example, when the dollar put/yen call option has much gamma, it means that the

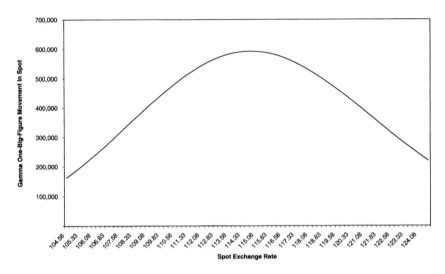

Exhibit 5.3a Gamma versus spot (USD put/JPY call: spot = 115; strike = 114.58; vol = 20.25%; R_d = 5%; R_f = 0.5%).

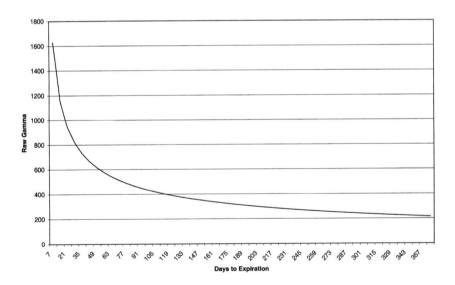

Exhibit 5.3b Gamma versus time (USD put/JPY call: spot = 115; strike = 114.58; vol = 20.25%; R_d = 5%; R_f = 0.5%).

option's delta will rise quickly with downward movements in the spot exchange rate, thereby allowing the holder of the option to capture progressively more profit. Conversely, the same option's delta will fall sharply with an upturn in the spot exchange rate, thereby limiting the size in the loss in the value of the option when spot moves adversely.

Theta

Theta (θ) is defined as the partial derivative of the option value with respect to the time remaining until expiration:

Theta

$$\theta_{call} \equiv \frac{\partial C}{\partial \tau} = -R_f e^{-R_f \tau} SN(x + \sqrt{\tau}) +$$

$$R_d e^{-R_d \tau} KN(x) + \frac{e^{-R_d \tau}\sigma}{2\sqrt{\tau}} KN'(x)$$

$$\theta_{put} \equiv \frac{\partial P}{\partial \tau} = R_f e^{-R_f \tau} S\big(N(x + \sqrt{\tau}) - 1\big) -$$

$$R_d e^{-R_d \tau} K\big(N(x) - 1\big) - \frac{e^{-R_d \tau}\sigma}{2\sqrt{\tau}} KN'(x)$$

The convention of the market is to express theta as the rate of *time decay* that will be experienced with the passage of one day. In the case of the dollar put/yen call from Exhibit 5.1, the daily time decay amounts to

$$\theta_{1\ day} = \frac{\theta_{call}}{365} \times FACE$$

$$\theta_{1\ day} = \frac{.0014143}{365} \times 1,145,800,000 = \$4,439$$

For a given time to expiration, theta takes on maximum value near the at-the-money-forward strike option (Exhibit 5.4a). Theta is sensitive to the amount of time remaining to expiration (Exhibit 5.4b). Options that have little time remaining to expiration experience the fastest rate of decay.

The passage of time can be understood in terms of the locus of option values in Exhibit 4.1. With the passage of time, the option

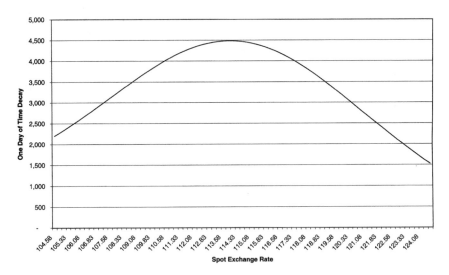

Exhibit 5.4a   Theta versus spot (USD put/JPY call: spot = 115; strike = 114.58; vol = 20.25%; R_d = 5%; R_f = 0.5%).

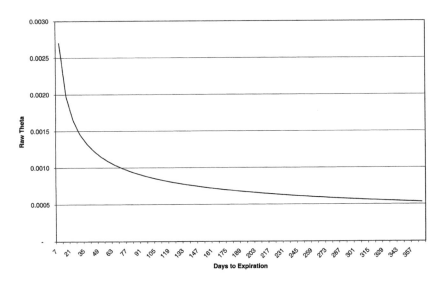

Exhibit 5.4b   Theta versus time (USD put/JPY call: spot = 115; strike = 114.58; vol = 20.25%; R_d = 5%; R_f = 0.5%).

curve drops toward the expiration locus. In the process, the curve sags, meaning that the option acquires additional convexity.

Some European currency options experience positive time decay, meaning that they gain value as time remaining to expiration decreases. If the foreign interest rate is sufficiently large relative to the domestic interest rate, an in-the-money call could experience positive time decay, meaning that the option might increase in value with the passage of time.

An example of positive time decay could be a European USD call/JPY put that is deep-in-the-money and where the dollar interest rate is very high relative to the yen interest rate. Given sufficiently low volatility, this option could become more valuable as time passes because that would mean less time to wait before the option holder receives possession of the higher-yielding domestic currency. Nonetheless, most European currency options experience negative time decay. Parenthetically, all American currency options experience negative time decay without exception because early exercise is permitted at any time in the option's life.

The passage of time can impact the value of a currency option in ways other than what theta would suggest. As time passes, an option is priced off a different part of the term structures of volatility and foreign and domestic interest rates. For example, the one-month option in Exhibit 5.1 is originally priced using one-month volatility and one-month interest rates. But one week later, the option, having only three weeks left to expiration, would be priced using three-week volatility and three-week interest rates. This could be material depending on the steepness or flatness of the term structures of volatility and interest rates.

Delta, Theta, and Gamma

Delta, theta, and gamma are related through the BSM partial differential equation. This equation (as introduced in Chapter 4) can be written

$$\frac{1}{2}\sigma^2 S^2 \gamma - R_d C + (R_d - R_f)S\delta - \theta = 0$$

where the symbols γ, δ, and θ, replace the partial derivatives, with no change in meaning. At a given level of delta, gamma and theta are directly related. This equation is the theoretical basis of why options with high levels of gamma have fast time decay, or as traders say, "theta is the rent on gamma."

Vega

An increase in volatility leads to increases in the value of all European options. This is because the greater the perceived level of volatility, the greater the probability that the option will expire in-the-money. The partial derivative of the option price with respect to volatility is given by *vega* (not a letter in the Greek alphabet).

Vega

$$vega_{call} = vega_{put} \equiv \frac{\partial C}{\partial \sigma} = e^{-R_d \tau} K \sqrt{\tau} N'(x)$$

Put and call vegas are equal for a common strike and expiration. Raw vega tells the change in option value for a 1 percent change in volatility (e.g., rising to 21.25% from 20.25%). Multiply raw vega by the option face and divide by 100 to arrive at the dollar change in the option. The raw vega for the dollar put/yen call in Exhibit 5.1 is .0009937, which makes the dollar sensitivity of the option equal to

$$\frac{vega}{100} \times face$$

$$\frac{.0009937}{100} \times 1,145,800,000 = \$11,386$$

Vega is at maximum value for a given expiration around the at-the-money-forward strike (Exhibit 5.5a). Unlike gamma and theta, vega is an increasing function of time to expiration (Exhibit 5.5b). The equation for vega indicates that option sensitivity to volatility increases with the square root of time to expiration.

Rho

The impact of domestic and foreign interest rates on option premium is somewhat subtle. In the framework of the risk-neutrality analysis, options are essentially probability-weighted discounted cash flows. Therefore an option's value is a function of the present

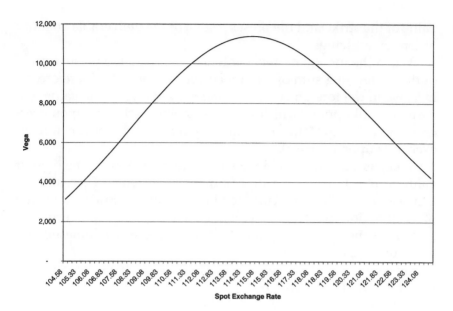

Exhibit 5.5a Vega versus spot (USD put/JPY call: 30 days; strike = 114.58; vol = 20.25%; R_d = 5%; R_f = 0.5%).

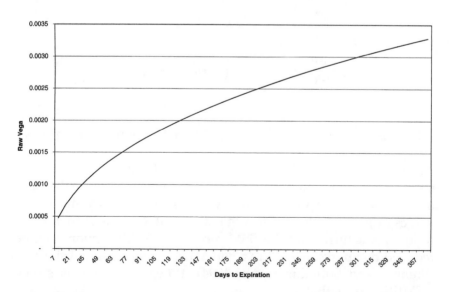

Exhibit 5.5b Vega versus time (USD put/JPY call: spot = 115; strike = 114.58; vol = 20.25%; R_d = 5%; R_f = 0.5%).

value of the strike and the present value of the deliverable quantity of foreign exchange.

When the foreign currency interest rate rises, the present value of the underlying sum of foreign currency must fall. Therefore, an increase in the foreign currency interest rate lowers the value of a currency call option (which receives foreign exchange upon exercise) and raises the value of a currency put (which delivers foreign exchange upon exercise).

Likewise, a rise in the domestic interest rate lowers the present value of the underlying sum of domestic currency. Therefore, an increase in the domestic currency interest rate will raise the value of a call option (which must pay domestic currency upon exercise) and lower the value of a put option (which receives domestic currency upon exercise).

By convention, the interest rate partial derivatives are called *rho* (ρ). The partials are given by

$$\frac{\partial C}{\partial R_d} = \tau e^{-R_d \tau} K N(x) \geq 0$$

$$\frac{\partial P}{\partial R_d} = \tau e^{-R_d \tau} K \left(N(x) - 1 \right) \leq 0$$

$$\frac{\partial C}{\partial R_f} = -\tau e^{-R_f \tau} S N(x + \sigma \sqrt{\tau}) \leq 0$$

$$\frac{\partial P}{\partial R_f} = -\tau e^{-R_f \tau} K \left(N(x \sigma \sqrt{\tau}) - 1 \right) \geq 0$$

Special Properties of At-the-Money-Forward Options

At-the-money-forward (ATMF) options are the most heavily traded currency options. Not surprisingly, traders favor them because these options have pure volatility value. They have near maximum values of gamma, theta, and vega among all options at their expiration. As it turns out, the BSM model for ATMF options can be reduced by approximation to a convenient computational shortcut (Brenner and Subrahmanyam, 1994). When an option is struck ATMF, it means that

$$K = F = Se^{(R_d - R_f)\tau}$$

which simplifies the arguments of the cumulative normal density function:

$$x = -\frac{\sigma}{2}\sqrt{\tau}$$

$$x + \sigma\sqrt{\tau} = \frac{\sigma}{2}\sqrt{\tau}$$

The value of the ATMF call or put becomes

$$C = P = e^{-R_f\tau}S\left[N\left(\frac{\sigma}{2}\sqrt{\tau}\right) - N\left(-\frac{\sigma}{2}\sqrt{\tau}\right)\right]$$

Kendall and Stuart (1943) state that the cumulative normal density $N(y)$ of variable y can be approximated as

$$N(y) = \frac{1}{2} + \frac{1}{\sqrt{2\pi}}\left(y - \frac{y^3}{6} + \frac{y^5}{40} - \cdots + \cdots\right)$$

For simplification to first approximation, we can drop the terms of third or higher order, whereupon

$$N(x) \cong \frac{1}{2} - .2\sigma\sqrt{\tau}$$

$$N(x + \sigma\sqrt{\tau}) \cong \frac{1}{2} + .2\sigma\sqrt{\tau}$$

The approximate value of the ATMF options becomes

$$C = P \cong 0.4e^{-R_f\tau}S\sigma\sqrt{\tau}$$

This approximation suggests that the value of the dollar put/yen call from Exhibit 5.1—which happens to be ATMF—is .0002019, which when multiplied by the yen face produces a total value of $231,276. This is reasonably close to the value of $230,827 from Exhibit 5.1. As an aside, note that the latter value was derived using a somewhat more precise yet less tractable approximation of the cumulative normal density function (see footnote 2 to Chapter 4).

A special rule of thumb for overnight options pops out of this approximation. Assuming that the foreign currency interest rate is not excessively high, the value of an overnight at-the-money call or put will be equal to .5 percent of the face value of the option if the quoted volatility is equal to 24 percent.

This approximation works tolerably well in the usual range of experienced currency option volatility (say, less than 50%). The same method provides simplifications for the ATMF deltas

$$\delta_{call} \cong e^{-R_f \tau} \left(\frac{1}{2} + .2\sigma \sqrt{\tau} \right)$$

$$\delta_{put} \cong e^{-R_f \tau} \left(.2\sigma \sqrt{\tau} - \frac{1}{2} \right)$$

Brenner and Subrahmanyam take matters one step further by approximating the normal density function

$$N'(x + \sigma \sqrt{\tau}) \cong 0.4$$

for values of the argument in the range normally experienced in option pricing. This allows for further simplification of ATMF gamma and vega:

$$\gamma \cong \frac{.4e^{-R_f \tau}}{S\sigma \sqrt{\tau}}$$

$$vega \cong 0.4e^{-R_d \tau} K \sqrt{\tau}$$

These approximations have proven useful to floor traders and market makers where there was a need to "trade on your feet" because of fast-moving markets.

Directional Trading with Currency Options

Directional trading involves taking positions consisting of spot and forward foreign exchange and options on foreign exchange that are designed to profit from correctly anticipating future movements in exchange rates. Directional trading is a risky business because foreign exchange rates can move violently and in unexpected ways. But when things work properly, directional trading can be explosively profitable.

Conventionally, trading in currencies is done in the spot market. A trader takes a position, either long or short, and waits for the anticipated move. Keeping exposure for longer than one foreign exchange trading day requires that the trader make arrangements to roll the position. To avoid the trader's having to make physical delivery, the position must be rolled out on the forward calendar using a forward swap transaction, such as tom/next or spot/next. Regardless of the exact method, being long a low-interest-rate currency (relative to the home currency) or short a high-interest-rate currency (relative to the home currency) involves paying interest-carrying charges. Conversely, being short a low-interest-rate currency (relative to the home currency) or long a high-interest-rate currency (relative to the home currency) pays the trader interest-carrying charges.

Most spot traders use stop-loss orders to protect themselves from adverse moves in exchange rates. An almost universal belief among traders is that some form of risk control is necessary lest they be caught the wrong way when a violent move in exchange rates occurs.

Trading currency options to catch directional moves in exchange rates is more complex than trading spot. New dimensions have to be considered in constructing trading positions. There is the placement of the option strike to consider and the choice of the option expiration. Option volatility has to be factored into the strategy.

All things considered, successful directional option trading involves more than a good prognostication of whether an exchange rate is going to go up or down in the future. Timing is important. The greatest profits come to the trader who is able to anticipate where the exchange rate will be at a specific future point in time. The best directional traders think simultaneously in the dimensions of direction, time, and volatility with a healthy appreciation for risk management.

ATMF Options and Wing Options

A trader who has a directional view must choose which option or options to use. Suppose that a trader is bearish on dollar/yen. Should he buy an at-the-money USD call/JPY put option, or a 25-delta yen put option (called the *wing* option) instead?

Exhibit 5.6 compares the instantaneous behavior of an ATMF USD put/JPY call (strike equal to 114.58) to that of a 25-delta yen call (strike equal to 110) using sensitivity analysis across exchange rates (traders call this a *slide*). The slide gives a bird's-eye view of how the value of the position and its risk characteristics would change if spot were to move up or down. Exhibit 5.6 moves spot up and down in increments of 2 yen, but this can be widened or shrunk.

The choice between the two options is not an easy one. What recommends the 114.58 strike option is its relatively high levels of delta and gamma at the initial spot level. The trader must pay commensurately more for this option than for the 110 strike option.

Volatility complicates the choice between the two options. As shown in Exhibit 5.6, at the initial spot level, the ATMF option has considerably more vega than the 25-delta option. In this exhibit, the quoted volatility for both the 114.58 and 110.00 strike options are assumed to be equal. Experience shows this to be a simplistic if not misleading assumption because low delta options often command extra volatility.

Initially the ATMF option has more delta, gamma, theta, and vega than the 25-delta option at the starting spot level of 115.00. However, if spot goes to lower levels, the 25-delta option will gradually become the new ATMF option, and the 114.58 strike option will lose some of its gamma, vega, and theta as it progressively goes deeper into-the-money.

The choice between the two options is not obvious, but the slide analysis at least affords a preview of either trade at hypothetical future spot levels.

Risk Reversals

One of the most aggressive directional trades is the risk reversal. A risk reversal is created by the purchase of an out-of-the-money option and sale of a directionally opposite out-of-the-money option.

An example of a risk reversal is a long position in a 25-delta USD put/JPY call combined with a short position in a 25-delta USD call/JPY put.

ATMF (strike 115.48)

	111	113	115	117	119
Theoretical value	$456,854	$331,592	$230,827	$153,694	$97,691
Delta	-$7,384,519	-$6,297,641	-$5,116,416	-$3,944,652	-$2,878,820
Gamma	$499,880	$570,250	$591,892	$561,691	$489,553
Vega	$9,619	$10,971	$11,386	$10,803	$9,414
Overnight decay	$4,124	$4,445	$4,440	$4,101	$3,506

25-delta (strike 110.00)

	111	113	115	117	119
Theoretical value	$204,409	$131,714	$80,653	$46,873	$25,840
Delta	-$4,746,294	-$3,552,674	-$2,503,873	-$1,659,702	-$1,034,506
Gamma	$612,080	$562,523	$472,169	$363,682	$258,184
Vega	$11,307	$10,390	$8,720	$6,715	$4,767
Overnight decay	$4,368	$3,915	$3,227	$2,452	$1,723

Exhibit 5.6 Comparison of ATMF option with 25-delta option ($10mm face, USD put/JPY call; vol = 20.25%; spot = 115; 30 days).

Risk Reversal

Long 25-delta 110 USD put/JPY call	$80,653
Short 25-delta 119 USD call/JPY put	($91,126)
Net premium	($10,473)

This trade is directionally bearish on the dollar. Assuming that the yen put and the yen call can be traded for approximately the same volatility, the risk reversal will be approximately zero cost initially.

If the view turns out to be correct, the value of the long yen call will rise and the value of the short yen put will fall. To an unsuspecting person this might look as though the trader had managed to acquire yen call for free. Yet any experienced option trader would scoff at the idea that the risk reversal is a free trade, even though it requires little or no up-front payment. The trade is not free because the short yen put is an at-risk position. If dollar/yen were to rise, the short yen put might cause a great deal of trouble.

This case can be seen in the top panel of Exhibit 5.7, where there is a slide of the risk-reversal trade. Note that at the onset, the delta of the risk reversal is approximately 50 in absolute value—the trade is long a 25-delta yen put and short a 25-delta yen call. The position is almost devoid of gamma, vega, and theta because of the offsetting effects of the long and short option positions.

When spot moves, the risk reversal begins to take on the personality of whichever option is favored. At lower levels of spot, the risk reversal becomes more like the long yen call as the importance of the short yen put recedes. But at higher levels of dollar/yen, the short call dominates. Accordingly, at lower levels of spot, the risk reversal will have positive vega, but at higher levels of spot, it will have negative vega.

It is important to realize that if the risk reversal goes bad, the trader will have a negative gamma position to hedge. Imagine the plight of a trader who tries to delta hedge this position when spot crisscrosses the strike of the short yen put. The trader will be caught having bought dollars right before the dollar drops and having to sell dollars right before the dollar rises. The only good outcome is the case where the trader buys dollars, preferably in the amount of the full face of the option, below the strike before the dollar rises without ever reversing. This raises the question as to whether it is

1-month 25-delta risk reversal (dollar bearish), $10mm face, strikes 110 and 119, vol 20.25%.

	109	112	115	118	121
Value	$287,175	$124,801	–$10,473	–$141,246	–$285,480
Delta	–$6,527,386	–$5,414,000	–$4,979,983	–$5,377,740	–$6,374,818
Gamma	$432,909	$275,160	$2,786	–$251,610	–$382,861
Theta	–$3,390	–$2,204	–$391	$1,178	$1,860
Vega	$7,738	$4,601	–$658	–$5,493	–$7,902

1-month vertical spread (dollar bearish), $10mm face, strikes 114.58 and 110, vol 20.25%.

	109	112	115	118	121
Value	$303,639	$226,062	$150,182	$88,228	$45,685
Delta	–$2,308,123	–$2,722,071	–$2,612,578	–$2,073,003	–$1,379,344
Gamma	–$208,584	–$53,230	$119,723	$220,362	$223,911
Theta	$909	–$142	–$1,212	–$1,753	–$1,655
Vega	–$3,549	–$568	$2,666	$4,476	$4,436

Exhibit 5.7 Direction trading with currency options.

ever advisable to use a risk reversal as a directional trade. The answer depends on one's risk appetite as well as one's trading agility. Professional foreign exchange traders do use risk reversals, but they have been known to experience some large losses, as well as some large profits, with this trade.

Vertical Spreads

A far less dangerous directional combination of options is the *vertical spread,* which consists of a long position in a put or a call plus a short position in a put or a call with a lower delta. Exhibit 5.7 (lower panel) contains a slide of the following vertical spread:

Vertical Spread

Long ATMF 114.58 USD put/JPY call	$230,835
Short 25-delta 110.00 USD put/JPY call	($80,653)
	Net premium $150,182

This vertical spread is directionally bearish on the dollar. The function of the short position in the 25-delta yen call is to lower the cost of the position. In turn, what is relinquished is any participation in directional gains below the 110.00 strike. The maximum gross profit on a $10,000,000 face spread is the difference between the strikes, which is equal to 4.58 yen, or $415,363. A directionally dollar bullish spread can be created by similar construction using yen puts.

Exhibit 5.7 shows that the vertical spread's greeks are muted at the initial spot rate of 115.00. Yet when spot approaches the vicinity of the short strike, the spread takes on the characteristics of the short option. This is caused simultaneously by the short strike option picking up sensitivity as it approaches its ATMF zone and by the long strike option losing sensitivity as it departs from its ATMF zone. Of particular interest is the fact that at the initial spot level, the vega of the spread is positive, but at lower spot levels the vega turns negative.

Vertical spreads are popular with technical traders who believe that they know precise levels where the spot exchange rate will meet support and resistance. The purpose of selling the lower-delta option is to unload an option that they think will expire worthless because spot will stop at a resistance level before the short strike. Nontechnical traders use vertical spreads to capture small- and medium-sized movements in exchange rates. The full power of the trade can be realized if the proceeds of the sale of the low-delta option are used to buy a larger position in the vertical spread.

Butterflies

No directional trade illustrates the importance of the relationship between time and direction in trading better than the *butterfly*. Suppose that spot dollar/yen is trading at 115.00 and that a trader has a 30-day trading target of 112.58, corresponding to a 2-yen downward move from the one-month forward of 114.58. A substantial amount of leverage with very little risk can be gained from the purchase of the following butterfly:

Butterfly

Long one 114.58 USD put/JPY call	$230,835
Short two 112.58 USD put/JPY call	($152,282)
Long one 110.58 USD put/JPY call	$94,023
	Net premium $20,294

The value at expiration is depicted in the following illustration:

The center or *body* of the butterfly is a short position in 112.58 yen call in double the face of the other options. The long positions in the 114.58 and 110.58 options are called the *wings*. The maximum expiration profit occurs at 112.58, where the 114.58 yen call is in-the-money by 2 yen, or $177,651, which is enormous compared to the investment of $20,294. Exhibit 5.8 shows a decomposition of the butterfly when 30 days remain to expiration.

	USD put/ JPY call	USD put/ JPY call	USD put/ JPY call	Butterfly
Position	1	–2	1	
Currency pair	USD/JPY	USD/JPY	USD/JPY	
Face $	$10,000,000	$10,000,000	$10,000,000	$10/$20/$10
Face JPY	1,105,800,000	1,125,800,000	1,145,800,000	
Spot	115.00	115.00	115.00	115.00
Strike	110.58	112.58	114.58	110.58/112.58/ 114.58
Days	30	30	30	30
Vol	20.25%	20.25%	20.25%	20.25%
Rd	5.00%	5.00%	5.00%	5.00%
Rf	0.50%	0.50%	0.50%	0.50%
Value	$94,023	$152,282	$230,835	$20,294
Raw delta	(28.00)	(39.20)	(51.16)	(0.76)
Delta	–$2,800,427	–$3,920,299	–$5,116,420	–$76,248
Gamma	$499,792	$570,399	$591,892	–$49,113
Theta	–$3,451	–$4,091	–$4,440	$291
Vega	$9,279	$10,781	$11,386	–$897
Raw delta	(0.28)	0.78	(0.51)	(0.01)

Exhibit 5.8   One-Month USD/JPY butterfly.

To appreciate the role of time, consider the value of the butter-fly at various times to expiration (Exhibit 5.9). Note that the but-terfly with 30 days to expiration is relatively insensitive to the spot level. The butterfly picks up sensitivity to spot as time to expiration decreases, and its final days are especially interesting. Right before expiration, the butterfly becomes highly sensitive to the level of the spot exchange rate when spot is anywhere close to the center strike.

Butterflies are peculiarly sensitive to volatility. When there is a great amount of time remaining to expiration, a butterfly will have an anemic level of vega (Exhibit 5.8). The butterfly picks up vega when little time is left before expiration and when it is positioned

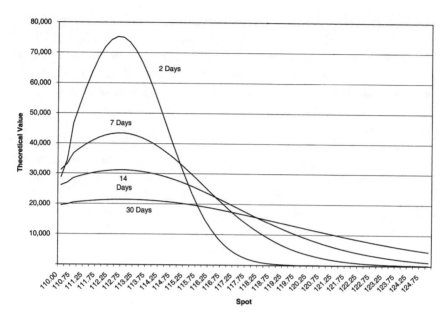

Exhibit 5.9   Butterfly (Dollar Bearish; Strikes at 110.58, 112.58, and 114.58).

over its *sweet spot,* meaning that the spot exchange rate is close to the center strike. Under this condition, the butterfly becomes a short-volatility trade, meaning that it is inversely sensitive to volatility. This is because a large movement in the spot exchange rate could knock the butterfly out of the money.

Hedging with Currency Options

Traditional currency hedging is done with forward contracts. Examples would be an exporter who sells foreign exchange forward to hedge expected foreign currency receipts and a portfolio manager who decides to hedge her holdings of foreign stocks or bonds by executing a series of rolling forward contracts (see DeRosa 1996).

Hedging with forwards has several complications, starting with the fact that the forward encapsulates the spread between the domestic and the foreign currency interest rates. Hence there is a cost to hedging a foreign currency that is at discount, meaning that the foreign interest rate is greater than the domestic interest rate. Conversely, a hedger is paid the interest rate spread when the foreign currency is at premium, meaning that the foreign currency has a lower interest rate than the domestic currency. This may be more of a concern to the exporter than to the portfolio manager because the latter's hedging costs might be recouped through future investment returns.

Operation of any currency hedging program involves the management of hedge-related cash flows. The accounting for foreign exchange hedging is the source of great confusion in many countries. For example, if a portfolio manager sells foreign exchange forward, and if the foreign currency being hedged appreciates, the hedging program will book a "loss." No actual, real loss will have occurred because the gains or losses in the hedging program will be matched by opposite currency translation losses and gains on the underlying portfolio. Yet not every country's accounting standards see it that way. In fact, the U.S. accounting for derivatives used in foreign currency hedging is still in a state of flux—witness the recent postponement of the introduction of the Financial Accounting Standards Board statement 133 ("Accounting for Derivative Dustruments and Hedging Activities") until after the millennium.

Hedging with currency options has similar concerns and requirements. Currency options, like forwards, are affected by interest rate spreads. Option hedging also has cash flow implications. Still, options do have natural advantages for hedgers. The exporter could "sell" his future foreign exchange receipts by purchasing a currency put. The portfolio manager could hedge his international portfolio by buying a strip of puts to cover each currency exposure in the portfolio.

The advantage one gets with an option is protection from losses that a hedger needs but with no sacrifice of potential benefits from upside movements in a foreign currency. The disadvantage is that options cost money to purchase. At times, quoted volatility is cheap and at other times it is dear.

The question that preoccupies hedgers is how to economize on the cost of option protection. There is no such thing as a free lunch. But it is possible for the hedger to mitigate the cost of buying options by selling other options that are of little value or no use to her. This brings us to an application of the risk-reversal trade that is very popular with exporters.

Take the case of a Japanese exporter who is owed a certain amount of dollars at a future date. The exporter wants to convert the dollars to yen at a future time but is worried that dollar/yen might fall in the meantime. If the exporter is willing to sacrifice some upside profit potential from possible upward movements in dollar/yen, then the trade for him to do is to buy a yen call and sell a yen put, both options being out-of-the-money-forward. The resultant structure, consisting of the long position in dollar/yen from the export activities, the long yen call, and the short yen put, is referred to as a *cylinder* or *collar*. Depending on the width of the spread between the option strikes, the exporter has room to participate in upward movements in dollar/yen but only as far as the strike of the yen put.

The most common risk-reversal construction uses 25-delta puts and 25-delta calls. Depending on market conditions, the premiums on the two options may be sufficiently close so as to offset each other completely. This transaction is often marketed to unsuspecting hedgers as being "costless." Although the collar transaction may be zero premium, meaning no up-front payment of cash is required, it is not costless because the potential appreciation in dollar/yen above the yen put strike has been surrendered to pay for the yen call. Moreover, there is a potential for loss, though it is limited, if dollar/yen drops because the "insurance" coverage does not start until the exchange rate dips below the strike on the yen call.

None of this is to say that collar trades are entirely ill advised. Rather, the point is that there is no free lunch in option hedging. Chapter 10 discusses some non–barrier option strategies that may prove useful to hedgers.

Appendix

Derivation of Delta

Deriving the partial derivatives of BSM equations requires only basic knowledge of differential calculus.

1. Calculus Rules

A few elementary calculus rules are required.

Polynomial Derivative Rule

$$\frac{d[ax^n]}{dx} = anx^{n-1}$$

Product Rule

$$\frac{d[uv]}{dx} = u\frac{dv}{dx} + v\frac{du}{dx}$$

Derivative of ln(x)

$$\frac{d\ln(x)}{dx} = \frac{1}{x}$$

Derivatives of e^x

$$\frac{d\,e^x}{dx} = e^x \text{ and } \frac{d\,e^u}{dx} = e^u\frac{du}{dx}$$

Derivative of the Cumulative Normal Density Function N(z)

$$\frac{dN(z)}{dx} = N'(z)\frac{dz}{dx}$$

where $N'(z)$ is the probability density function defined as

$$N'(z) = \frac{1}{\sqrt{2\pi}} e^{-\frac{z^2}{2}}$$

Also note the following property:

$$N(-x) = 1 - N(x)$$

2. The BSM Model Is As Follows:

$$C = e^{-R_f \tau} S N(x + \sigma\sqrt{\tau}) - e^{-R_d \tau} K N(x)$$

$$P = e^{-R_f \tau} S \left[N(x + \sigma\sqrt{\tau}) - 1 \right] - e^{-R_d \tau} K \left[N(x) - 1 \right]$$

$$x = \frac{\ln\left(\frac{S}{K}\right) + \left[R_d - R_f - \frac{\sigma^2}{2} \right] \tau}{\sigma\sqrt{\tau}}$$

3. Two Intermediate Partial Derivatives:

The following derivatives are used repeatedly in the analysis that follows.

$$\frac{\partial x}{\partial S} = \frac{\partial}{\partial S} \left[\frac{\ln S}{\sigma\sqrt{\tau}} - \frac{\ln K}{\sigma\sqrt{\tau}} + \frac{\left(R_d - R_f - \frac{\sigma^2}{2} \right) \tau}{\sigma\sqrt{\tau}} \right] = \frac{1}{S\sigma\sqrt{\tau}}$$

$$\frac{\partial (x + \sigma\sqrt{\tau})}{\partial S} = \frac{1}{S\sigma\sqrt{\tau}}$$

4. A Useful Result:

$$e^{-R_f \tau} S N'(x + \sigma\sqrt{\tau}) = e^{-R_d \tau} K N'(x)$$

This is easily proved as follows:

$$\frac{N'(x)}{N'(x + \sigma\sqrt{\tau})} = \frac{e^{-\frac{x^2}{2}}}{e^{\frac{-(x+\sigma\sqrt{\tau})^2}{2}}} = e^{x\sigma\sqrt{\tau}+\frac{1}{2}\sigma^2\tau} = e^{\ln(\frac{S}{K})+(R_d-R)\tau} = \frac{Se^{-R_f\tau}}{Ke^{-R_d\tau}}$$

5. Finally, Solve for the Deltas:

Call Delta

$$\frac{\partial C}{\partial S} = e^{-R_f\tau}N(x + \sigma\sqrt{\tau}) + e^{-R_f\tau}SN'(x + \sigma\sqrt{\tau})\frac{\partial(x + \sigma\sqrt{\tau})}{\partial S}$$

$$- e^{R_d\tau}KN'(x)\frac{\partial x}{\partial S}$$

The partials in the second and third terms both equal

$$\frac{1}{S\sigma\sqrt{\tau}}$$

The second and third terms cancel, leaving

$$\frac{\partial C}{\partial S} = e^{-R_f\tau}N(x + \sigma\sqrt{\tau})$$

Put Delta

$$\frac{\partial P}{\partial S} = -e^{-R_f\tau}N(-(x + \sigma\sqrt{\tau})) - e^{-R_f\tau}SN'(-(x + \sigma\sqrt{\tau}))\frac{\partial(-(x + \sigma\sqrt{\tau}))}{\partial S}$$

$$+ e^{R_d\tau}KN'(-x)\frac{\partial(-x)}{\partial S}$$

Similar to the case of the call delta, the second and third terms in this equation cancel, leaving

$$\frac{\partial P}{\partial S} = e^{-R_f \tau} \left(N(x + \sigma \sqrt{\tau}) - 1 \right)$$

One can solve for all of the other BSM partial derivatives in a similar manner, using these basic rules of differential calculus.

Chapter **6**

Volatility

The Various Meanings of Volatility

The term *volatility* is ubiquitous in the option markets. Yet volatility has several distinct meanings depending on whether the context is the behavior of the spot foreign exchange rate or concepts related to option pricing.

Theoretical Volatility

One of the core assumptions of the Black-Scholes option-pricing theory is that instantaneous changes in the spot exchange rate follow the following diffusion process:

$$\frac{dS}{S} = \mu dt + \sigma dz$$

The term dz is defined as a Gaussian white-noise process that has zero mean and standard deviation equal to $\sqrt{dt}$. σ is assumed to be a known constant, known as *theoretical volatility*. Volatility enters the theoretical value of an option through this parameter.

Actual Volatility

Actual volatility refers to the behavior of percentage changes in a spot exchange rate. The actual volatility of a known history of an exchange rate is called the *historical volatility* over some relevant time frame. Sometimes reference is made to the future behavior of a spot exchange rate; this is called *prospective* or simply *future volatility*.

Actual volatility is the sample standard deviation of percentage rates of return of the spot exchange rate over a period of time. The rate of return of the spot exchange rate, R_t, is calculated as the first log differences in the spot rate:

$$R_t \equiv \ln(S_t) - \ln(S_{t-1}) = \ln\left(\frac{S_t}{S_{t-1}}\right)$$

where S_t and S_{t-1} are successive observations on the spot exchange rate (expressed in American convention). The unbiased sample standard deviation, $\hat{\sigma}$, is given by

$$\hat{\sigma} = \sqrt{\frac{1}{n-1}\sum_{t=1}^{n}(R_t - \bar{R})^2}$$

where there are n observations in the sample and $\bar{R}$ is the sample mean. An alternative statistic, which is thought to be more statistically efficient (but biased), is given by

$$\hat{\sigma}' = \sqrt{\frac{1}{n-1}\sum_{t=1}^{n}R_t^2}$$

Parkinson (1980) proposes alternative estimators. Parkinson's extreme value method uses the natural log ratio of the day's high and low spot exchange rates:

$$\hat{\sigma}_p = \sqrt{\frac{.361}{n}\sum_{t=1}^{n}\ln\left(\frac{High_t}{Low_t}\right)^2}$$

The annualized standard deviation can be found by multiplying by the square root of the number of days in the sample period. Some practitioners use a 365-day count (calendar standard deviation), whereas others prefer to use the numbers of trading days in one year, roughly 252 days.

Implied Volatility

In the context of option-pricing theory, volatility is a Black-Scholes parameter that is an input used to calculate the theoretical value of an option. But in some trading environments, such as with exchange-traded options, an actual market price is known for options. It is possible to reverse the BSM model to extract what volatility is "implied" by the known money price using Newton's algorithm for finding the roots of a polynomial. An initial guess of the implied volatility is made to start the procedure. This value is plugged into the BSM model to give an initial estimate of the option price, which can be compared to the actual known option price. The difference, which is called the *error*, is used to calculate a new candidate volatility using the following formula:

$$\sigma_{n+1} = \sigma_n + \frac{C - C(\sigma_n)}{vega(\sigma_n)}$$

where σ_{n+1} is the candidate volatility on the $(n + 1)$th iteration, σ_n is the candidate volatility from the previous iteration, C is the known value of the option, $C(\sigma_n)$ is the value of the call implied from the previous candidate volatility, and the option vega, meaning the partial derivative of the option price with respect to volatility, is as follows:

$$vega(\sigma_n) = e^{-R_d \tau} K \sqrt{\tau} N'(x)$$

In usual practice, this algorithm converges on a reasonably precise estimate of implied volatility in three or four iterations.

For the special case of at-the-money-forward options, implied volatility can be approximated using the Brenner and Subrahmanyam technique presented in Chapter 5:

$$\hat{\sigma} \cong \frac{2.5C}{e^{-R_f \tau} S \sqrt{\tau}}$$

Quoted Volatility

In the interbank currency option market, traders make currency option prices in terms of *quoted volatility*, which is subsequently changed into a money price using the BSM model. Quoted volatility is actually a form of implied volatility. But in the context of the interbank currency option market, the implied volatility of an option is known in advance of the money price of the option, hence the distinction quoted volatility. Yet although option traders sometimes distinguish quoted volatility from implied volatility, there is not often a meaningful difference between the concepts.

Exhibit 4.3 from Chapter 4 displayed examples of quoted volatility on major currencies observed in January 1999. Note that volatility varied widely across currencies and exhibited differences across term to expiration. The quoted volatilities in Exhibit 4.3 apply to at-the-money-forward options.

Quoted volatility is anything but constant across time. Exhibit 6.1 displays daily observations on one-month quoted volatility for options on dollar/yen as observed in the period July 1994 to April 1999. One-month volatility was rarely above 15 percent, except during some parts of 1995 and during a spectacular episode of exchange rate volatility in the autumn of 1998. Exhibit 6.1 also shows one-year quoted volatility on dollar/yen. Note that the "volatility of volatility" is inversely related to the term to expiration; the

Exhibit 6.1   Quoted volatility on dollar/yen, one-month and one-year, July 1994 to April 1999, weekly observations. *Source:* The RiskMetrics Group. Reprinted with permission.

volatility of long-term quoted volatility is smaller than that of short-term quoted volatility. Exhibit 6.2 shows quoted volatility for dollar/mark for options of one month and one year.

It is interesting to ask what happens to quoted volatility in a currency crisis. In the spring and summer of 1997, the Southeast Asian currency crisis erupted, starting with a speculative attack on the Thai baht. In May 1997, the Bank of Thailand reacted by aggressively selling dollars and buying baht. Moreover, it instructed domestic Thai banks to cease lending baht to overseas customers (presumed to be the speculators), thus creating a two-tier currency market for the baht. The bank won the immediate battle but soon lost the war. On July 2, 1997, the Bank of Thailand was forced to float the baht. Exhibit 6.3 shows one-month quoted volatility on dollar/baht. Quoted volatility rose swiftly as the crisis became manifest. Volatility continued to climb as the crisis spread from one country to the next throughout the region and remained at relatively high levels until late of 1998.

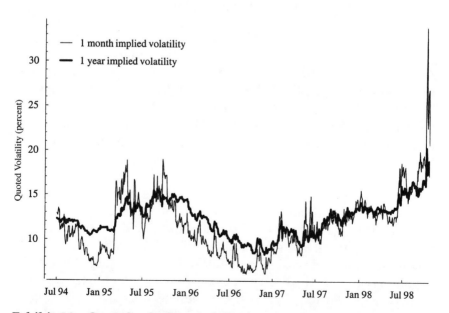

Exhibit 6.2   Quoted volatility on dollar/mark, one-month and one-year, July 1994 to April 1999, weekly observations. *Source:* The RiskMetrics Group. Reprinted with permission.

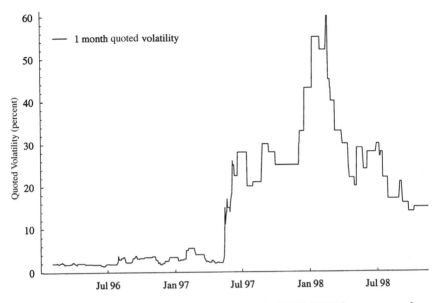

Exhibit 6.3   Quoted volatility on dollar/baht (USD/THB), one-month, January 1995 to December 1998, monthly observations. *Source:* The RiskMetrics Group. Reprinted with permission.

Another interesting period was the summer and autumn of 1992, when the European Monetary Union experienced the so-called sterling crisis. Exhibit 6.4 displays the behavior of the sterling/ mark exchange rate taken from Malz (1996). Sterling entered the Exchange Rate Mechanism (ERM) in October 1990 at a central rate against the mark of 2.95 marks. Sterling was permitted to fluctuate inside a bandwidth equal to ±6 percent around its ECU central rate. Crucial for sterling was its relationship to the mark because the latter served as the anchor of the exchange rate grid. Sterling was forced out of the ERM on September 2, 1992.

Exhibit 6.5 (1996) shows the behavior of one-month and one-year sterling/mark quoted volatility. Quoted volatility declined following sterling's admission to the ERM. However, quoted volatility began to rise sharply as early as October 1991, which later was recognized as a warning sign that trouble was ahead. The crisis that followed began to take shape on June 3, 1992, when the Maastricht treaty, an essential component of the ultimate single-currency project, was defeated by a Danish referendum.

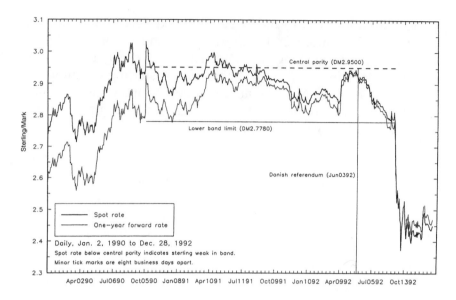

Exhibit 6.4 The sterling/German mark exchange rate in the ERM. *Source:* Reprinted from *Journal of International Money and Finance,* Allan Malz, 1996, with permission from Elsevier Science.

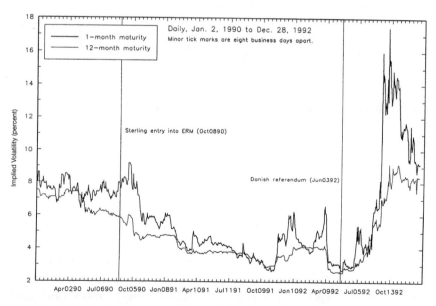

Exhibit 6.5 Sterling/mark at-the-money implied volatility. *Source:* Malz (1996). *Source:* Reprinted from *Journal of International Money and Finance,* Allan Malz, 1996, with permission from Elsevier Science.

The sterling crisis formed over the next several months, climaxing on September 2, 1992, when sterling encountered irrepressible waves of selling pressure. The story did not end there, however. Once free of the ERM constraints, sterling continued to plunge violently against the mark in the course of the week that followed. Things finally settled down in October, whereupon quoted option volatility began to drop.

The Volatility Term Structure

The term structure of implied or quoted option volatility can assume any shape whatsoever; it can be positive sloping, negative sloping, or flat. Xu and Taylor (1994) studied the behavior of implied volatility from the Philadelphia Stock Exchange currency options on pounds, marks, Swiss francs, and yen during the period 1985 to 1990. They report:

> The term structure sometimes slopes upwards, sometimes downwards, and its direction (up or down) frequently changes. The direction changes, on average, approximately once every two or three months. . . . The term structures of the pound, mark, Swiss franc, and yen at any moment in time have been very similar. (73)

As a general rule, implied volatility rises whenever there is a good reason to believe that a sharp movement in spot rates is probable, as in the cases of the Thai baht in 1997 and during the sterling ERM crisis of 1992. Short-dated options are usually well bid in such an environment because they are rich in gamma. But when the excitement fades, short-dated volatility has been known to move quickly to lower levels.

Implied volatility can possess a subtle yet ephemeral relationship with the level of the spot exchange rate. Traders have a nickname for this phenomenon, *dollar-voler*, because it was first identified as a relationship between the levels of the dollar and implied and quoted volatilities of dollar calls and puts. A good example is dollar/yen in 1994, when the spot rate broke below the 100 level for the first time. The Bank of Japan publicly expressed concern that the yen had appreciated too much against the dollar. The view in the market was that if the dollar were to sink any lower, the Bank of Japan, and possibly other central banks, would intervene to buy dollars against yen. These concerns were reflected in the pricing of dollar/yen options. The level of implied volatility rose for short-dated expirations. More interesting was the fact that a relationship between the level of the spot rate and implied volatility became ingrained into the market. Implied volatility rose whenever the dollar fell against the yen but reversed itself whenever the dollar rose.

Forward Volatility

As has been discussed, quoted or implied volatility in the currency option market has an observable term structure. It is natural to wonder whether expectations of future volatility play any part in how the market prices short- and long-term-dated options. There is a direct parallel between this question and the classical theory of the term structure of interest rates. For example, *forward volatility* can be extracted from the term structure of volatility much the same way as forward interest rates can be obtained from the term structure of interest rates.

Because volatility is linear in its square (i.e., variance), we can define the forward volatility as follows: Suppose we observe the term structure at various equally spaced points on the term structure and there are observed volatilities σ_1 and σ_2 corresponding to maturities τ_1 and τ_2 with $\tau_1 < \tau_2$. The long-term volatility can be decomposed as follows:

$$\tau_2 \sigma_{t_2}^2 = \tau_1 \sigma_{t_1}^2 + (\tau_2 - \tau_1)\sigma_{t_1,t_2}^2$$

where σ_{t_1,t_2} is defined as the forward volatility. For example, if three- and six-month quoted volatility were 10 percent and 15 percent, respectively, the three-month forward volatility would be

$$\sqrt{\frac{\left[.5 \times (15\%)^2 - .25 \times (10\%)^2\right]}{.25}} = 18.71\%$$

Campa and Chang (1998) investigated whether interbank forward quoted volatility has any predictive power for future quoted volatility. They studied daily quoted volatility for options of up to one year in term on four major currencies over the period December 1989 to May 1995. Campa and Chang cannot reject the expectations hypothesis that quoted volatility predicts future quoted volatility. In other words, they detect a relationship between current short-term volatility, current long-term quoted volatility, and future short-dated quoted volatility. They conclude:

> In sharp contrast to the literature on the term structure of interest rates, we conclude that for all currencies and maturity pairs, current spreads between long-run and short-run volatility do predict the right direction of future short-rate and long-rate changes, even at horizons that are as brief as one month. (90–91)

Campa and Chang perform out-of-sample tests to determine whether forward volatility is a good predictor of future actual volatility in spot exchange rates. For most of their sample period, December 1989 to July 1993, forward volatility is an inferior predictor of future quoted volatility to forecasts from Box-Jenkins time series models (see Box and Jenkins, 1970).

Smiles, Risk Reversals, and the Implied Volatility Surface

It is a well-known empirical finding that out-of-the-money options can trade at higher implied volatilities than same-expiration at-the-money options. The same phenomenon is often evident in equity and equity-index options.

The best explanation of the *smile* is the well-documented empirical observation that sample currency return distributions exhibit departures from the theoretical normal distribution. In the BSM model, currency returns are assumed to be normally distributed. Any number of empirical investigations show that sample currency returns are leptokurtic, meaning that relative to the theoretical normal population, the sample is peaked and there is a greater frequency of extreme outlier values. Given the elevated occurrence of outliers, low delta options ought to be attractive to traders who seek low-cost, high-leverage, speculative trades.

The smile in quote currency option volatility is often nonsymmetrical (hence the term *crooked smile*). Traders call this the *volatility skew*. It can be measured by comparing the quoted volatility on same-delta calls and puts, most commonly in reference to the 25-delta calls and 25-delta puts at one-month or three-month term to option expiration. Note that option-pricing theory requires that same-strike puts and calls trade at the same quoted volatility (for a common expiration); this is merely an exercise in put-call parity. However, there is no theoretical reason, much less any arbitrage rule, that forces the quoted volatilities for same-delta out-of-the-money options to be equal.

Risk reversals were introduced in the previous chapter as directional trades and as components of foreign exchange hedging strategies. From the dealer's perspective, a risk reversal exchanges a call for a put or a put for a call (Malz 1998). For example, suppose that a dealer quotes the one-month dollar/yen 25-delta risk reversal as ".50 to 1.50 for yen calls over yen puts." In the risk-reversal market, quotes are given in volatility terms relative to some mid-level volatility. Assuming a midlevel volatility of 14.50, the dealer's quote means that he is willing to (1) buy a USD put/JPY call for 15.00 and sell the USD call/JPY put for 14.50, or (2) sell a USD put/JPY call for 16.00 and buy the USD call/JPY put for 14.50. Said another way, the dealer is 14.50 "choice" for the yen put and makes a bid-ask price of 15.00–16.00 for the yen calls. Parenthetically, dealers use the term *around* to quote a risk reversal with no preference for calls over puts or puts over calls.

Skew can change from one day to the next. Institutional factors can be the reason for the skew in some currencies. Dollar/yen is a prime example. Japanese exporters are naturally long dollars, which they intend to convert to yen at some time. One of the favorite trades of the exporters is the collar transaction described in the previous chapter. Exporters buy an out-of-the-money dollar put/yen call and sell an out-of-the-money dollar call/yen put for zero or near-zero cost. The combination of the risk reversal with their long dollars creates the *collared* long dollar position.

The term *implied volatility surface*[1] refers to observations of quoted volatility across term structure and strike structure dis-

---

1. The implied volatility surface is not to be confused with a related concept of the local volatility surface. Each point on the implied volatility surface is the implied volatility that can be entered into a Black-Scholes formula and have the option theoretical value equal its current market price. Embedded in the implied volatility surface is a local volatility specific to every possible future spot level and future time. The local volatility surface can be extracted from the implied volatility surface. The origins of this concept come from Derman and Kani (1994b), Dupire (1994), and Rubinstein (1994).

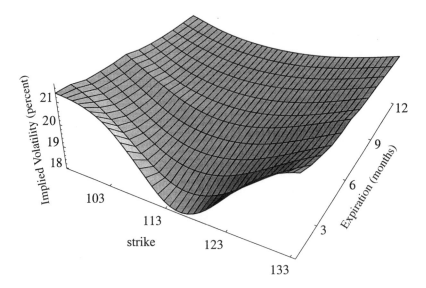

Exhibit 6.6 Implied volatility surface for dollar/yen, March 1, 1999.
Source: The RiskMetrics Group. Reprinted with permission.

played in three dimensions (see Derman, Kani, and Zou 1995). The
implied volatility surface for dollar/yen in March 1999 is shown in
Exhibit 6.6. The metric for "moneyness" is the delta of the yen call
options, but some traders draw the volatility surface with call
deltas on the left-hand side and put deltas on the right-hand side
centered around the 50-delta strike. These two representations are
essentially equivalent because the sum of the call and put deltas is
given by

$$\delta_{call} - \delta_{put} = e^{-R_f \tau}$$

which for short-term expirations and low foreign interest rates is
close to unity.

Risk-Neutral Densities

The Cox-Ross risk-neutral approach presented in Chapter 4 establishes that the value of an option is equal to the present value of the
conditional expectation of the spot exchange rate at expiration
minus the strike. The mathematical expectation is conditional on the

option being in-the-money at expiration. Observed market prices for currency options therefore imply a set of risk-neutral probability densities for the future spot exchange rate.

Malz (1997) explores methods for extraction of risk-neutral probability distributions of future exchange rates from observed quoted volatilities of currency options at differing terms and strikes. Exhibit 6.7 is the risk-neutral density function for dollar/yen as observed in March 1999, which is consistent with the volatility surface depicted in Exhibit 6.6 (both exhibits were generously provided by Dr. Malz of the RiskMetrics Group to the author). A slight risk-reversal skew is implied by the distribution in Exhibit 6.7, revealing a slight bias for yen puts over yen calls.

More interesting yet is the implied probability density function on sterling/mark during the famous ERM crisis in 1992 (Exhibit 6.8, Malz 1996). Malz describes it as follows:

> The distribution is tight and centered at high values of F_t, $t + \tau$ (the forward outright) in the spring of 1992. As sterling weakens and the

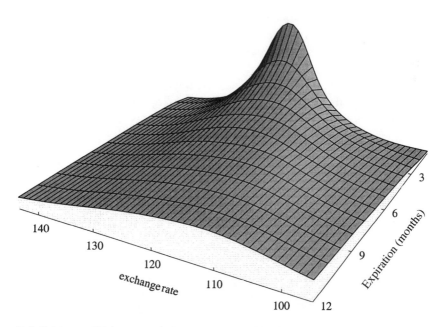

Exhibit 6.7 Risk-neutral densities on dollar/yen, March 31, 1999.
Source: The RiskMetrics Group. Reprinted with permission.

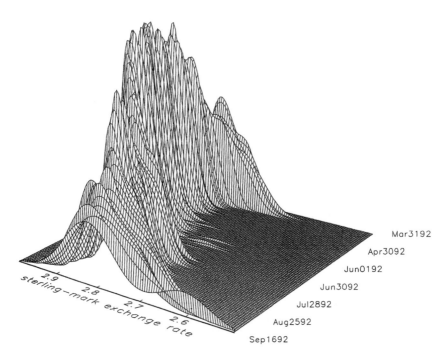

Exhibit 6.8 Probability density function of the sterling/mark exchange rate. *Source:* Reprinted from *Journal of International Money and Finance,* Allan Malz, 1996, with permission from Elsevier Science.

> credibility of the target zone dissolves, the distribution becomes more dispersed and its centre moves lower. For days on which the market price of protection against realignment risk was high, but the estimated variance was low, the distribution is bimodal. (735)

Malz's comment on the bimodal nature of the implied distribution at the crescendo of the crisis, in September 1992, means that the relative price of deep-out-of-the-money options on sterling/mark became exorbitant as the market came to realize that sterling's days in the ERM were about to end.

Dealing in Currency Options

As was mentioned earlier, currency option market making is concentrated in a small group of money-center banks that have active foreign exchange desks. The objective of the currency option dealer is to capture an *edge,* meaning to earn the bid-ask spread by making a market in options, without taking significant financial risk.

Newcomers to the field often incorrectly presume that currency option dealers are in the business of turning trades between buyers and sellers. In other words, it is supposed that the dealer looks to sell an option at the asking price to a customer after having bought the same option at the bid from a different bank customer. This is not how this business functions. Dealers buy and sell currency options on a hedged basis and then warehouse their option trades in a collective option book. A large option dealer might have thousands, and in some cases tens of thousands, of currency options in its book.

Dealers sort their option books by currency pairs, for example, dollar/yen or euro/dollar, for ease of hedging. They manage directional risk in two stages. First, they buy and sell options with the accompaniment of spot foreign exchange hedges, as was described in Chapter 4. This practice turns option trades for dealers into delta-neutral events. The second stage is an ongoing process of managing the subsequent directional risk of the option book as a whole by performing rebalancing transactions in spot foreign exchange. The objective of these rehedging trades is to keep the aggregate delta of the option book flat so as to avoid the risk associated with movements in the spot exchange rate. The aggregate delta, gamma, and theta of a currency option book are the summation of the delta, gamma, and theta of the individual component currency options for a specific currency pair.

The implied economies of scale should be noted. A large currency option book is likely to have a variety of puts and calls held as both long and short positions. Hence there is a natural consolidation of the option's book exposure by virtue of offsetting positions. The practical implication is that there is less need to do rehedging trades in order to maintain the book in a flat delta state. This reason alone accounts for some of the oligopolistic industrial structure of the currency option business.

Vega is more complicated. It makes no sense to sum the vegas of options of differing terms because quoted volatility does not move in parallel shifts across its term structure. Short-term volatility is more volatile than long-term volatility.

Some dealers get around this problem by slicing the option book into *time buckets.* Each bucket contains all of the options that fall into a narrow interval of term to expiration, such as in the range between six months and one year. Inside of each bucket, vega can be aggregated with little loss of meaning.

Another method applies regression analysis to historical time series of implied volatility across term to expiration to estimate *weighted vega*. Weighted vega is centered around a chosen term to expiration, six months being popular. The purpose of this exercise is to standardize vega across the option portfolio. The vegas of longer-term options are thus deflated in proportion to the observed relative magnitude of the fluctuations in quoted volatility at their respective expirations. Weighted vega is additive across the option portfolio for a given currency pair.

In a similar manner, option risk associated with interest rates is complicated by nonparallel shifts in interest rate term structures. Fortunately, interest rate risk is not usually material for options with terms of less than one year, at least not compared to the risk from movements in spot exchange rates and volatility. Yet interest rate risk, or *rho risk,* can dominate all other pricing factors in currency options that have multiyear lives. For this reason, it is common for dealing banks to assign long-term currency options to their interest rate product risk managers.

Extensions of the BSM Model

The universal finding that sample spot exchange rate returns are leptokurtic has led to the development and testing of new currency option–pricing models. One such model is the *stochastic variance model,* where the variance of the spot exchange rate is introduced as a random variable. A second new model is the *jump process model,* which assumes that currency returns are driven by the mixture of a diffusion process and a jump process.

The Stochastic Variance Model

One explanation for the sample leptokurtosis is that time-varying parameters might drive exchange rates. In particular, variance might obey a stochastic process all of its own apart from the process that generates the spot exchange rate. Treating volatility as a stochastic variable resolves the disturbing conflict between theory and practice when traders quote option volatility as a moving price.

The problem is that volatility itself cannot be traded directly in the marketplace. Hence, volatility could command a risk premium that would have to enter the option partial differential equation explicitly.

Chesney and Scott (1989) apply to currency options a stochastic variance model originally developed by Hull and White (1987), Scott (1987), and Wiggins (1987). Their objective is to price European currency options in an environment where variance is allowed to behave as a random variable. In the stochastic variance model, the spot exchange rate follows one stochastic process,

$$\frac{dS}{S} = \mu dt + \sigma dz_1$$

and volatility follows a second stochastic process,

$$\frac{d\sigma}{\sigma} = \left[\frac{1}{2}\gamma^2 + \beta[\alpha - \ln \sigma]\right] dt + \gamma dz_2$$

where z_1 and z_2 are assumed to be independent and β, α, and γ are constants. The natural logarithm of σ is mean reverting by design.

The Chesney and Scott model assumes no correlation between volatility and exchange rate returns and that interest rates are constant and riskless over the option's life. The model is as follows:

The Stochastic Variance Currency Option Model

$$C(S, \sigma, \tau) = \int_0^\infty \left[e^{-R_f \tau} S N(d_1) - e^{-R_d \tau} K N(d_2)\right] d\hat{F}(\bar{V})$$

$$d_1 = \frac{\ln\left(\frac{S}{K}\right) + \left(R_d - R_f + \frac{1}{2}\bar{V}\right)\tau}{\sqrt{\bar{V}}}$$

$$d_2 = d_1 - \sqrt{\bar{V}}$$

$$\bar{V} = \frac{1}{\tau}\int_t^T \sigma_S^2 \, dS$$

where $\bar{V}$ represents the mean variance of the instantaneous movements in the spot rate over the life of the option and $\hat{F}$ is the distribution function of $\bar{V}$. The value of a currency put can be derived from the currency call under the put-call parity theorem.

Part of the motivation for going to the stochastic variance model is to correct the observed anomaly that on a relative basis the BSM model overprices at-the-money-forward options and under-prices options with low deltas. Stochastic variance models, starting with the Hull and White model, do not have this defect.

Unfortunately, there is no easy way to apply the stochastic volatility option model. Chesney and Scott use Monte Carlo simu-lation to compare the BSM model to the stochastic volatility model. The BSM model is done two ways, one with a constant variance for exchange rates and the other in which the variance is allowed to be reestimated daily. Their sample consisted of observations on prices on European calls and puts on dollar/Swiss franc collected from a major dealing firm in Geneva. Chesney and Scott conclude:

> We find that the actual prices on calls and puts conform more closely to the Black-Scholes model if we allow the variance rate to be revised every day. When we use a constant variance rate, we find that the Black-Scholes model performs very poorly. Even though we find that the Black-Scholes model outperforms the stochastic variance model, we do find much evidence from both the option prices and the foreign exchange rate series to support the notion that volatility changes ran-domly. (283)

The Mixed Jump-Diffusion Process Model

Sample leptokurtosis could be an artifact of exchange rate returns being generated by a mixed jump-diffusion process. In such a process, a time series follows a diffusion process but is subject to random jumps. The jumps themselves are governed by still another stochastic process. For example, the process governing exchange rates might be specified as

Mixed Jump-Diffusion Model

$$\frac{dS}{S} = \mu dt + \sigma dz + dq$$

The first two terms on the right-hand side are the diffusion process components and the third term, dq, is the jump process component. The jump component can be modeled as a Poisson process; it could be described by two parameters, the mean number of jumps that take place in a unit of time and the expected size of one jump, Y. The actual jumps, Y_i, are assumed to be independent and lognormally distributed.

In discrete time, the currency return can be written as

$$\ln \frac{S_t}{S_{t-1}} = \mu + \sigma z + \sum_{t=1}^{n_t} \ln Y_i$$

where n_t is the actual number of jumps during a particular interval.

Jorion (1989) finds important evidence of the existence of significant discontinuous jumps in sample foreign exchange returns. Moreover, the stochastic variance model cannot account for these discontinuities. Like Hsieh (1989), Jorion uses the first-order autoregress conditional heteroscedastic (ARCH) model to represent a time-varying variance process. This model takes the form of a process in which the next observation is conditional on available information from the prior periods:

$$x = \ln \frac{S_t}{S_{t-1}} \mid_{t-1} = \mu + \sqrt{h_t} z$$

where

$$h_t = \alpha_0 + \alpha_1 (x_{t-1} - \mu)^2$$

where x_{t-1} is the prior period's currency return and α_1 is the autoregressive parameter introducing heteroscedasticity.

Jorion tested weekly and monthly currency returns on the German mark, British pound, and Japanese yen over the period from January 1974 to December 1985. In monthly data, he found weak evidence that allows him to reject a pure diffusion process in favor of a jump-diffusion process and to reject a pure diffusion process in favor of an ARCH model. However, the results are more definitive in weekly data. Here, the jump-diffusion process is a significant improvement over a simple diffusion process. Of the total variance of the German mark, 96 percent is accounted for by the jump process component and only 4 percent by the diffusion process component. Moreover, the jump-diffusion process is shown to be a superior description of the sample in comparison to the ARCH model.

For comparison, Jorion repeats the same tests on a value-weighted index of New York and American Stock Exchange common stocks. The jump component for stocks is not nearly as significant as it is for exchange rates. Jorion writes,

> Maximum-likelihood estimation of a mixed jump-diffusion process reveals that exchange rates exhibit systematic discontinuities, even after allowing for conditional heteroscedasticity in the diffusion process. The results are much more significant in the foreign exchange market than in the stock market, which suggest differences in the structures of these markets. (27)

Presumably, Jorion would have found more evidence of a jump component in the U.S. stock market had his sample not stopped short of the 1987 and 1989 market dislocations. Nonetheless, the idea of a jump process has more intuitive appeal for foreign exchange markets, which are subject to frequent coordinated central bank interventions.

Jorion explores the size of the bias in the BSM model, derived from a simple diffusion process, relative to Merton's (1976) jump process option-pricing model as adapted for currency options. Merton's model, which assumes that jump risk does not command an economic risk premium in the market, is as follows:

Merton's Model Adapted for Currency Options

$$C_{Merton} = e^{-R_f \tau} \sum_{j=0}^{\infty} \frac{e^{-\lambda \tau e^{\theta + .5\delta^2}} (\lambda \tau e^{\theta + .5\delta^2})^j}{J!}$$

$$\times C \left(S, \tau, R_d - R_f + j \frac{\theta + .5\delta^2}{\tau} - \lambda(e^{\theta + .5\delta^2} - 1), \sigma_0^2 + j\frac{\delta^2}{\tau}, K \right)$$

where σ_0^2 is the variance of the diffusion component of the process, λ is the mean number of jumps per one interval, and δ^2 is the variance of the jump size Y. Note that the total variance of the mixed jump-diffusion process is given by

$$\sigma^2 = \sigma_0^2 + \lambda\delta^2$$

Jorion's principal concern is a finding by Bodurtha and Courtadon (1987) that diffusion models seriously underprice short-term out-of-the-money options by as much as 29 percent. Jorion explains the relevance of jump processes to this problem:

> If the exchange rate follows a diffusion process, the chance of exercising the option at maturity may be quite small; with a jump process, however, one jump may be sufficient to move the option in the money, which implies that a diffusion model will underprice the option. (439)

Of the total under-pricing of short-term out-of-the-money options of the 29 percent reported in Bodurtha and Courtadon, Jorion believes that 17 percent can be explained by failing to account for the jump process component of exchange rates.

One important question is whether either the stochastic volatility or mixed jump-diffusion models can explain the observed volatility smile. In theory, either model could account for the phenomenon of the symmetric smile. Taylor and Xu (1994) are able to trace a portion of the smile to stochastic volatility. Taking the analysis further, Bates (1994) creates a *nested* stochastic volatility/jump-diffusion model that he tests with trading data on the IMM deutsche mark futures options. Bates reports,

> The stochastic volatility sub-model cannot explain the "volatility smile" evidence of implicit excess kurtosis, except under parameters implausible given the time series properties of implied volatilities. Jump fears can explain the smile, and are consistent with one 8% DM depreciation "outlier" observed over the period 1984–91. (69)

Trading Volatility

Option traders speak of being long or short volatility when they take positions hoping to correctly anticipate future quoted or actual volatility. In the most basic sense, any position that is long a put or a call is long volatility. Options are *long quoted volatility* in the sense that their value will rise if quoted volatility rises. Options are also *long actual volatility* because greater fluctuations in the spot exchange rate mean that there is a greater chance of expiring in-the-money.

Straddles

The classical volatility trade is to go long volatility by buying a straddle or short volatility by selling a straddle. A *straddle* is the combination of same-strike puts and calls. Parenthetically, a synthetic straddle can be created by adding a spot foreign exchange hedge to a put or a call in the size of the option delta.

Long straddle positions benefit from large movements in the spot exchange rate in either direction. A sufficiently large movement could compensate for the cost of straddle premium. Long straddles also rise in value when implied volatility rises and falls in value when implied volatility falls.

A short straddle is a short volatility trade. It appreciates when there is little or no movement in the spot exchange rate and when implied volatility drops. A short straddle, however, can produce dangerous losses if exchange rates suddenly exhibit violent fluctuations.

Gamma Scalping

Option traders have figured a way to trade actual volatility against implied volatility through a process called *gamma scalping*. The concept is suggested by the Black-Scholes methodology. Suppose that the implied volatility of one-month euro/dollar options is quoted at 8.35 percent, but the trader is convinced that actual volatility in the euro over the next month will be much larger. This view can be expressed by purchasing a one-month option (either a put or a call or even a straddle) and operating a dynamic hedging strategy using spot foreign exchange.

In theory, with no frictions or transaction costs, the dynamic hedging program to a first approximation would recoup the original option premium if the actual volatility over the option's life were to match the original 8.35 percent implied volatility. If actual volatility were to materialize at a higher level than 8.35 percent, there would be a profit to the strategy because the gains from the dynamic hedging program would exceed the cost of buying the option. Conversely, if actual volatility were to turn out to be lower than 8.35 percent, the program would produce a net loss.

The reason that the hedging program generates cash can be understood from Exhibit 6.9, where a gamma scalping program is operated over three days in volatile and calm market environ-

1. EUR/USD Volatile Market

	Day 1	Day 2	Day 3	Total
Spot	1.0579	1.0679	1.0579	
Days to expiry	30	29	28	
Option value (USD)	$94,859	$147,695	$91,014	
Delta (USD)	–$5,028,652	–$6,565,100	–$5,005,271	
Daily time decay		$1,905	$1,951	$3,856
Hedge	$5,028,652	$6,565,100	$5,005,271	
Daily P&L hedge		–$47,534	$61,477	$13,943
Daily P&L option		$52,836	–$56,681	–$3,845
Total P&L		$5,302	$4,796	$10,098

2. EUR/USD: Calm Market

	Day 1	Day 2	Day 3	Total
Spot	1.0579	1.0599	1.0579	
Days to expiry	30	29	28	
Option value (USD)	$94,859	$102,717	$91,014	
Delta (USD)	–$5,028,652	–$5,336,220	–$5,005,271	
Daily time decay		$1,939	$1,951	$3,890
Hedge	$5,028,652	$5,336,220	$5,005,271	
Daily P&L hedge		–$9,507	$10,069	$562
Daily P&L option		$7,858	–$11,703	–$3,845
Total P&L		–$1,649	—$1,634	–$3,283

Exhibit 6.9 Gamma scalping. One-month USD put/EUR call: $10mm USD face, strike = 1.06, vol = 8.35%, R (USD) = 4.922%, R(EUR) = 2.571%.

ments. On day 1, a $10 million face USD put/EUR call with 30 days to expiration is purchased for $94,859. This option is hedged by going long $5,028,652 in spot foreign exchange. In the top panel, the volatile market case, spot euro dollar rises overnight from 1.0579 to 1.0679 (by "one big figure"). At the new spot rate, the option rises by $52,836 but the spot hedge loses $47,534—there is a net profit overnight equal to $5,302. Now the delta has risen and the hedge is expanded to $6,565,100. On day 3, the spot exchange rate falls back to its original level of 1.0579. The overnight loss on the option is equal to $56,681, but the hedge earns $61,477 for a daily net profit of $4,796.

A very different picture is seen in the second panel, where the overnight movement in the spot is more modest, from 1.0579 to 1.0599, or by 20 pips. This magnitude of movement in the spot exchange rate is not sufficient to recover the overnight decay in the value of the option, and the program loses money over the two-day period.

Yet in both market environments, hedging by itself makes money over the two-day period. More to the point, note that the spot exchange rate in the exhibit does a round trip back to its original level. The reason that the hedging earns money is that the size of the hedge is dynamically adjusted to mimic the delta of the option. Delta changes, and by extension so does the size of the hedge, with movements in spot. These changes are predicted by the second derivative of the option theoretical value with respect to the spot exchange rate, the gamma. Hence the program is called gamma scalping.

In Black-Scholes terms, the process of operating the dynamic hedge amounts to synthetically selling the option at the actual volatility. Yet this is an exaggeration because the actual time path of the spot exchange rate is merely described but not uniquely determined by the standard deviation.

What is not shown in the exhibit is a case where implied volatility changes in the course of the program. In the volatile market case, it is not out of the question that implied volatility might rise if traders come to expect that more big moves in the spot exchange rate will follow. If implied volatility were to rise to the target level that the trader had established for actual volatility, then the trader would have an opportunity to terminate the program ahead of schedule. In effect, the rise in the value of the option would capture the profit that had been anticipated from the gamma scalping exercise. On the other hand, if implied volatility were to drop, the option profit and loss account would suffer.

Mixing Directional and Volatility Trading

In some market environments, implied volatility is predictable by movements, or even levels, in the spot exchange rate. This can create very powerful trading opportunities where both a directional view and a volatility view can be combined in one strategy.

Dollar/yen is a prime example, to continue themes discussed earlier. Suppose that the level of spot USD/JPY is equal to 110 and that it is known that the Bank of Japan does not want further appreciation in the yen. Suppose that a trader has a three-month target for USD/JPY to fall to 100. Moreover, let's hypothesize that he thinks that the Bank of Japan will put up a fight before the dollar falls to 100. As a general rule, sudden intervention by a central bank causes option implied volatility to rise. Therefore, an ideal way to express both views is to buy USD put/JPY call options with strikes around the 100 level and terms to expiration at three months or more. The trader stands to profit on both the directional move and the rise in implied volatility.

Yet in a larger sense, every option trade that is not fully delta-hedged is a mixed direction and volatility trade. Sometimes, volatility movements can nullify directional gains or even compound directional losses on trades.

Chapter **7**

American Exercise Currency Options

American currency options allow exercise at any time before expiration. Some interbank currency options and most listed currency options feature American exercise privilege.

Arbitrage Conditions

American exercise privilege results in arbitrage conditions that differ from those implied by European exercise. Denote American currency calls and puts as C' and P', respectively.

Immediate Exercise Value

The minimum value of an in-the-money American option is equal to the value of immediate exercise:

$$C' \geq S_t - K$$
$$P' \geq K - S_t$$

for all times in the life of the option, $0 \leq t \leq T$.

Time Value

The value of an American option is a positive function of its remaining time to expiration, all other things being equal:

$$C'(T - t_0) \geq C'(T - t_1)$$
$$P'(T - t_0) \geq P'(T - t_1)$$

where $(T - t_0)$ and $(T - t_1)$ are times to expiration and $t_1 > t_0$. Because exercise is permitted at any time before expiration, a reduction in the remaining time to expiration has a negative effect on the value of American calls and puts. This result is not always true for European options.

American and European Exercise

The minimum value of an American option is an European option. That is,

$$C' \geq C$$

$$P' \geq P$$

A complete lower bound for American options is obtained by combining the immediate exercise value with the lower bound for European exercise options (from Chapter 4):

$$C' \geq Max\lfloor 0, S - K, e^{-R_f \tau} S - e^{-R_d \tau} K \rfloor$$

$$P' \geq Max[0, K - S, e^{-R_d \tau} K - e^{-R_f \tau} S]$$

Put-Call Parity for
American Currency Options

The put-call parity theorem for European currency options states that

$$P - C = e^{-R_d \tau} K - e^{-R_f \tau} S$$

For American currency options put-call parity takes the form of an inequality:

$$C' + K - Se^{-R_f \tau} \geq P' \geq C' + Ke^{-R_d \tau} - S$$

The left-hand side of the inequality

$$C' + K - Se^{-R_f \tau} \geq P'$$

must hold at expiration because a portfolio combination consisting of

a. Long call C'

b. $\$K$ invested in a zero coupon bond that matures at option expiration with value $Ke^{+R_d\tau}$

c. A short position in a foreign currency zero coupon bond that pays one unit of foreign exchange at expiration that is worth S_T

will be worth more at expiration than the put by an amount equal to

$$Ke^{+R_d\tau} - K \geq 0$$

regardless of where the spot exchange rate is relative to the strike. This can be verified with the following analysis of the values at expiration of going long the portfolio and short the put:

Value before expiration	Value at expiration $S_T > K$	$S_T < K$
C'	$S_T - K$	0
$+K$	$e^{+R_d\tau}K$	$e^{+R_d\tau}K$
$-e^{-R_f\tau}S$	$-S_T$	$-S_T$
$-P'$	0	$-(K - S_T)$
	$e^{+R_d\tau}K - K$	$e^{+R_d\tau}K - K$

This guarantees that the left-hand side of the inequality must hold if the combination is held to expiration. Next, what is needed is to show that it must hold allowing for the possibility of early exercise. If the inequality did not hold, the inverse condition,

$$C' + K - S_e^{-R_f\tau} \leq P'$$

would be true, which would mean that we could sell the put for more than we would have to pay to buy the portfolio combination. This condition is impossible, even with early exercise. If the holder of the put did elect to exercise, we would be obligated to pay $\$K$ and receive one unit of foreign exchange worth S. To pay $\$K$, we could liquidate the domestic currency bond. This bond would be worth more than $\$K$, so we would be able to pocket some accrued interest. Also, the deliverable one unit of foreign exchange would give us more than enough to repay the short position in the foreign currency zero coupon bond, so again there would be a positive residual. On top of this, the long position in the call would have a nonnegative value. All things counted, the inverse condition cannot be valid because it implies that a costless, riskless, and valuable position would be available in the market.

Likewise, the right-hand side

$$P' \geq C' + Ke^{-R_d\tau} - S$$

must also hold at expiration because a portfolio combination consisting of

a. Long call C'
b. Long zero coupon bond that matures at expiration with value $\$K$ (present value $Ke^{-R_d\tau}$)
c. A short position in a foreign currency zero coupon bond with present value equal to one unit foreign exchange

will be worth less than the value of the put at expiration by the amount

$$S_T e^{+R_f\tau} - S_T \geq 0$$

A similar argument can be made as to why the right-hand side of the parity inequality must hold even in the case of early exercise. If it were not valid, the inverse condition

$$P' \leq C' + Ke^{-R_d\tau} - S$$

would hold, and it can be shown that this is impossible by virtue of the no-arbitrage condition. If the inverse condition were true, a profitable arbitrage trade could be done by buying the put and selling the more expensive combination, the latter consisting of

a. Short call C'
b. Short a zero coupon bond that matures at expiration with value $\$K$ (present value $Ke^{-R_d\tau}$)

c. A long position in a foreign currency zero coupon bond that pays one unit foreign exchange at option expiration

If the call were exercised before expiration, we would be obligated to deliver one unit of foreign exchange worth $S and receive domestic currency in the amount of the option strike, $K. Because the short position in the domestic currency zero coupon bond has a present value less than K, we would pocket some domestic currency. Also, we would be able to liquidate the foreign currency zero coupon bond for more than one unit of foreign exchange and keep some accrued interest there as well. Furthermore, we own the put, which has a nonnegative value. Altogether, the inverse condition of the right-hand side of the put-call inequality cannot hold because it implies that a costless, riskless, but valuable trade is available in the market.

General Theory of American Currency Option Pricing

The Black-Scholes methodology was specifically developed for European exercise options, yet it does have some insights to offer about American exercise options. Working with the same set of assumptions that underlie the BSM European exercise currency option model, assume that

1. There are no taxes, no transaction costs, and no restrictions on taking long or short positions in either options or currency. All transactors in capital and foreign exchange markets are price takers. This means that no single economic agent can buy or sell in sufficient size so as to control market prices.
2. The foreign and domestic interest rates are riskless and constant over the term of the option's life. All interest rates are expressed as continuously compounded rates.
3. Instantaneous changes in the spot exchange rate are generated by a diffusion process of the form

$$\frac{dS}{S} = \mu dt + \sigma dz$$

where μ is the instantaneous drift and dt is an instant in time, σ is the instantaneous standard deviation, and dz is the differential of a stochastic variable that is normally distributed with mean zero and standard deviation equal to the square root of dt.

Option pricing theory states that these assumptions are sufficient to derive the Black-Scholes partial differential equations for any currency option, including American exercise currency puts and calls. The equations are:

$$\frac{1}{2}\sigma^2 S^2 \frac{\partial^2 C'}{\partial S^2} - R_d C' + (R_d - R_f)S\frac{\partial C'}{\partial S} - \frac{\partial C'}{\partial \tau} = 0$$

$$\frac{1}{2}\sigma^2 S^2 \frac{\partial^2 P'}{\partial S^2} - R_d P' + (R_d - R_f)S\frac{\partial P'}{\partial S} - \frac{\partial P'}{\partial \tau} = 0$$

For European options, the payoffs at expiration are governed by

$$C_T = max[0, S_T - K]$$
$$P_T = max[0, K - S_T]$$

As described in Chapter 4, Black and Scholes, and later Garman and Kohlhagen, used these expiration payoff functions as boundary conditions in the solution of the partial differential equations for European call and put options.

American options are governed by different boundary conditions because early exercise is permitted. American options are constrained to never be worth less than zero or worth less than their intrinsic value:

$$C_t = max[0, S_t - K]$$
$$P_t = max[0, K - S_t]$$

where t denotes the current time. These conditions must hold at every point in time in an American option's life. No analytic solution to the partial differential equations, using the American boundaries, is known to exist. Consequently, option theoreticians have turned to other classes of model. Some are numerical procedures, like the binomial model of Cox, Ross, and Rubinstein (1979), and others are analytical approximations, such as the compound option model of Geske and Johnson (1984), the quadratic approximation model of MacMillan (1986) and Barone-Adesi and Whaley (1987); and Ho, Stapleton, and Subrahmanyam (1994).

The Economics of Early Exercise

American currency puts and calls are commonly exercised before expiration. A sufficient condition for early exercise is that an American option sell for less than its intrinsic value:

Sufficient Conditions for Early Exercise

$$C' < S_t - K$$
$$P' < K - S_t$$

For an American call, the *opportunity cost* of early exercise is the foregone interim interest that could have been earned by investing the present value of the strike for the days between a candidate exercise date and expiration. This is equal to

$$K(1 - e^{-R_d \tau})$$

On the other hand, the opportunity cost of not electing early exercise for the call is the interim interest that could be earned by investing the present value of the deliverable one unit of foreign exchange for the days between a candidate exercise date and expiration. This is equal to

$$S(1 - e^{-R_f \tau})$$

The net difference of these two expressions can be thought of as the *interest opportunity cost* of the option.

Gibson (1991) notes the following necessary but not sufficient condition for early exercise of an American call:

Necessary Condition for Early Exercise: American Call

$$S(1 - e^{-R_f \tau}) > K(1 - e^{-R_d \tau})$$

Early exercise depends not only on the option's in-the-moneyness but also on the spread between the domestic and foreign interest rates.

This analysis shows why early exercise of an American currency call is likely to be optimal for options deep-in-the-money and where the foreign currency interest rate is high relative to the domestic interest rate. The condition is necessary but not sufficient, because even if the interest opportunity cost were large, the option might still be worth keeping alive at sufficiently high levels of volatility. In other words, the interest opportunity cost might be more than offset by the chance that the option will be carried even deeper-in-the-money by a big move in the exchange rate. This statement takes on added importance if spot exchange rates contain a jump process component.

For an American put, the necessary condition for optimal early exercise is given by the inequality

Necessary Condition for Early Exercise: American Put

$$K(1 - e^{-R_d\tau}) > S(1 - e^{-R_f\tau})$$

For American currency puts, optimal early exercise is likely to occur when the option is deep-in-the-money and when the foreign currency interest rate is below the domestic interest rate. Optimal exercise of an American put requires that the interim interest that can be earned on the strike between a candidate exercise date and expiration exceed the interim interest on the deliverable quantity of foreign exchange. This is a necessary but not sufficient condition because at sufficiently high levels of volatility, the volatility value of the put might be worth more than the interest opportunity cost. The exact conditions under which it is optimal to choose early exercise depend on the in-the-moneyness of the option, the foreign and domestic interest rates, and volatility.

Currency option traders make early-exercise decisions in terms of the following paradigm. Consider whether to exercise an in-the-money put. As was described in Chapter 4, the value of an in-the-money put can be decomposed into three parts—parity to the forward, a present value factor, and the volatility value of the option. The volatility value of the in-the-money put is equal to its pure *optionality*, which, according to the put-call parity theorem, is equal to the value of the same-strike out-of-the money call (which we will designate as $\bar{C}'$).

Exercising the in-the-money put causes three things to happen:

a. The option holder receives the benefit of the interest differential between the two currencies from the time of exercise to the expiration date of the option (time interval τ). This is worth

$$K(1 - e^{-R_d\tau}) - S(1 - e^{-R_f\tau})$$

b. The option holder is released from paying the cost of carry associated with the premium of the option, which can be written

$$R_d\tau P'$$

c. The exercise kills the volatility value of the put, which is captured in the value of the same-strike call, $\bar{C}'$.

If the sum of a and b is greater than c, it is optimal to exercise the option at some time before expiration. In other words, if the value of early exercise is positive, exercise is indicated. We can write

Value of Early Exercise: American Put

$$\left(K(1 - e^{-R_d\tau}) - S(1 - e^{-R_f\tau})\right) + R_d\tau P - \bar{C}'$$

The value of early exercise for a dollar call/yen put plotted against the spot exchange rate is displayed in Exhibit 7.1. The option parameters behind this exhibit are:

Option	USD call/JPY put
Face (USD)	$10,000,000
Face (JPY)	1,150,000,000
Exercise	American
Strike	115.00
Days to expiry	90
USD interest rate	7.00%
JPY interest rate	0.50%
Volatility	20.00%

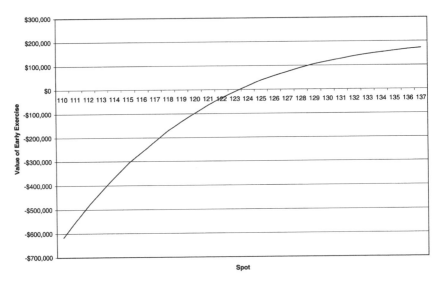

Exhibit 7.1   Early exercise of American USD call/JPY put—term decision.

Exhibit 7.1 indicates that early exercise at some time in the life of the option is optimal at spot exchange rates above 124.00; this is known as the *term decision.*

A second condition controls whether early exercise is immediately optimal. This takes into consideration the overnight level of market interest rates and the overnight volatility value of the option. At an assumed spot level of 124.00, the value of a one-day dollar call/yen put represents the overnight volatility value of a one-day in-the-money dollar put/yen call. To see if early exercise is optimal today, compare that overnight volatility value to the overnight interest advantage and the overnight carry on the option. If the condition for exercise is not met, the option would be better exercised at a later time.

Exhibit 7.2 demonstrates that the overnight exercise rule is a function of short-term market option volatility. At a high enough level of overnight volatility, over 66 percent, the dollar call/yen put is best left unexercised for one day—even though the term decision rule has established that early exercise is optimal at some point in time. This is particularly relevant around significant market event times, when overnight volatility has been known to spike upward.

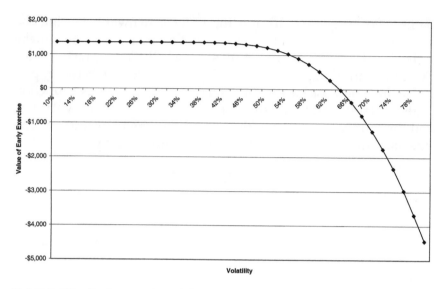

Exhibit 7.2 Early exercise of American USD call/JPY put—overnight decision.

Under normal circumstances, early exercise that is indicated by the term decision will be confirmed by the overnight rule. But in some cases, where there is a potential market-rocking event, such as a central bank meeting, an election, or a G-7 meeting, early exercise could optimally be delayed. Taleb (1997) provides advanced discussion of the difficulties of implementing mechanical early-exercise decision rules.

The Binomial Model

Cox, Ross, and Rubinstein (1979) propose the binomial option model as an alternative to the Black-Scholes model. The binomial model can value both European and American options on common stocks that pay dividends, and it explicitly recognizes the possibility of early exercise. Bodurtha and Courtadon (1987) modify the binomial model to work on currency options.

The Binomial Paradigm

In the binomial model, the spot exchange rate at a point in time is constrained to jump in one of two possible mutually exclusive paths; one being upward and the other downward. During the remaining time to expiration, τ, the spot exchange rate must make a fixed number, N, of such jumps, which the user must specify. Practically speaking, the choice of N is a compromise between precision and speed of calculation. The size of each jump is a function of the domestic and foreign interest rates, the assumed volatility, and the number of jumps in the remaining time to expiration. The size of an up jump u and a down jump d are given by

$$u = e^{(R_d - R_f)\frac{\tau}{N} + \sigma \sqrt{\frac{\tau}{N}}}$$

$$d = e^{(R_d - R_f)\frac{\tau}{N} - \sigma \sqrt{\frac{\tau}{N}}}$$

Let the superscript that precedes a variable denote the sequence number of the jump. After the first jump, the initial spot rate S_0 will either be "up," designated ^1S_u, or "down," designated ^1S_d:

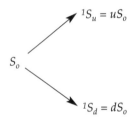

For purposes of example, we will work with the paradigm of a USD put/JPY call:

Option	USD put/JPY call
Underlying asset	1 yen
Strike	.0087275 (= 1/114.58)
Spot	.0086956 (= 1/115.00)
Days to expiry	30
Interest rate (USD)	5.00%
Interest rate (JPY)	0.50%
Volatility	20.25%

To begin with the simplest case, let the spot exchange rate be constrained to make only one jump between time 0 and day 30.

This means that N equals 1 and that the magnitude of the up and down jumps, u and d, would be equal to

$$u = e^{(5.00\% - 0.50\%)\frac{30}{365} + 20.25\%\sqrt{\frac{30}{365}}} = 1.0637002$$

$$d = e^{(5.00\% - 0.50\%)\frac{30}{365} - 20.25\%\sqrt{\frac{30}{365}}} = 0.9470946$$

Accordingly, the spot exchange rate on day 30, S_T, would be either

$$S_T = {}^1S_u = uS_0 = 1.0637002 \times .0086956 = .0092496$$

or

$$S_T = {}^1S_d = dS_0 = 0.9470946 \times .0086956 = .0082356$$

Furthermore, on day 30, the value of the call would have only two possible expiration values, depending on whether spot had moved up or down:

Up
$${}^1C_u = Max[0,\ {}^1S_u - K] = 0.00052204$$

or

Down
$${}^1C_d = Max[0,\ {}^1S_d - K] = 0$$

where ${}^1C_u$ and ${}^1C_d$ are the values of the call that are conditional upon respective up and down movements in the spot exchange rate.

From these meager bits of information, the value of the call option on day 0 can be deduced without knowing in advance the direction of the jump of the spot exchange rate. This is because a portfolio with known market value at time 0 can be constructed to exactly replicate the value of the call at expiration. This portfolio consists of a combination of (1) a borrowed quantity, B, of dollars with repayment promised on day 30, and (2) a purchased quantity, D, of spot yen. Assuming that arbitrageurs can borrow and lend at the rates R_d and R_f, the future value of the borrowed dollars at expiration is equal to

$$Be^{R_d \tau}$$

The dollar value of the spot yen at time zero is $S_0 D$. Interest on the yen will accrue at the rate of R_f. The future dollar value of the yen will be equal to either

$$^1 S_u De^{R_f \tau} = u S_0 De^{R_f \tau}$$

or

$$^1 S_d De^{R_f \tau} = d S_0 De^{R_f \tau}$$

where the only unknown is the future spot exchange rate.

The values of B and D that replicate the call are given by the following formulas

$$B = \frac{u\, {}^1C_d - d\, {}^1C_u}{(u-d)e^{R_d \tau}} = -.004222728$$

$$D = \frac{{}^1C_u - {}^1C_d}{(u-d)S_0 e^{R_f \tau}} = .5146045$$

The expiration-day value of this portfolio does in fact exactly match that of the call:

Call (^1C_u and ^1C_d)		Portfolio	
Up	.00052204	Dollar loan $Be^{R_d \tau}$	(0.004240118)
		Value of yen $S_u De^{R_f \tau}$	0.004762158
		Total	0.00052204
Down	0	Dollar loan $Be^{R_d \tau}$	(0.004240118)
		Value of yen $S_d De^{R_f \tau}$	0.004240118
		Total	0.0

This means that the value of the call at time zero must equal the known market value of the portfolio; otherwise riskless arbitrage would be profitable. The value of the call then must be

$$C_0 = B + S_0 D = 0.000252406$$

Seen another way, from the risk-neutral argument of Cox and Ross (1976), the value of C_0 can be represented as the risk-neutral expected present value of the binomial pair of outcomes

$$C_0 = e^{-R_d \tau} \left[p^1 C_u + (1 - p)^1 C_d \right]$$

where p is the risk-neutral probability of an upward move and $(1 - p)$ is the risk-neutral probability of a downward move. The former can be obtained by rearranging the terms of $C_0 = B + S_0 D$ equation with p defined as

$$p = \frac{e^{(R_d - R_f) \tau} - d}{(u - d)}$$

The Binomial Tree Structure

Now we will consider the case of two jumps before expiration ($N = 2$ and ($\tau/N = 0.0410959$). The magnitude of the up and down jumps is given by

$$u = e^{(5\% - 0.50\%) \frac{1}{2} \times \frac{30}{365} + 20.25\% \times \sqrt{\frac{1}{2} \frac{30}{365}}} = 1.0438339$$

$$d = e^{(5\% - 0.50\%) \frac{1}{2} \times \frac{30}{365} - 20.25\% \times \sqrt{\frac{1}{2} \frac{30}{365}}} = 0.9615567$$

The tree structure for the spot exchange rate becomes

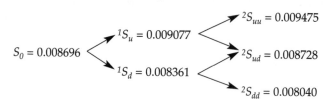

and the payoff pattern for the call in abstract can be depicted as

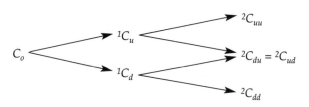

At expiration, there are exactly $N + 1$ possible terminal values for the call option. Each of them is either in-the-money, and worth $S_T - K$, or worthless. In the $N = 2$ case there are three expiration values:

$$^2C_{uu} = .00074716$$

$$^2C_{du} =\ ^2C_{ud} = .00000035$$

$$^2C_{dd} = 0$$

The binomial model starts with expiration values and works "backward" toward time 0. First, the set of nodes that is one jump before expiration is evaluated. Each of these nodes has a binomial pair of outcomes. For example, at the ^1C_u node in the $N = 2$ case, the option will advance to either $^2C_{uu} = .00074716$ or $^2C_{ud} = .00000035$, which can be found by examining the fragment of the tree structure

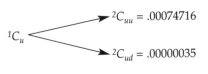

Using the procedure of replicating this payoff pattern by borrowing dollars and buying yen, we can calculate that B is equal to $-.00870961$ and D is equal to $.9997945$. The value of ^1C_u is the greater of zero and the value of the portfolio consisting of short dollars and long yen or the immediate exercise value,

$$^1C_u = Max\lfloor 0,\ B +^1 S_u D,^1 S_u - K \rfloor$$

$$= Max[0,\ .00036453,\ .0003493] = .00036534$$

The same procedure must next be used for ^1C_d, which finds this node's value equal to $.00000017$.

Finally, the value of C_0 can be found to be $.00017864$, utilizing the same replication procedure of borrowing dollars and purchasing yen now that we know the binomial pair of outcomes, ^1C_d, and ^1C_u.

$$C_o \quad \begin{cases} {}^1C_u = .00036534 \\ {}^1C_d = .00000017 \end{cases}$$

The General Binomial Model

Two jumps, of course, are not enough to accurately value an option. A great many more are required for accuracy. Using 50 jumps, the binomial model values the American option at .00020428 (or $234,065 per $10 million of face). But no matter how large N is, the procedure is always the same: First evaluate the expiration values; next, move back one jump to the $(N-1)$th node; continue until the entire binomial tree has been calculated to produce C_0.

In the generic case, say, at node n, the call value at the node can be found as

$$Max\lfloor 0, {}^nB + {}^nS\,{}^nD, {}^nS - K \rfloor$$

where the final term in the brackets, ${}^nS - K$, represents the sufficient condition for early exercise. At each generic node n, the values of ${}^nB$ and ${}^nD$ are given by

$$
{}^nB = \frac{u\,{}^{n+1}C_d - d\,{}^{n+1}C_u}{(u-d)e^{R_d \frac{\tau}{N}}}
$$

$$
{}^nD = \frac{{}^{n+1}C_u - {}^{n+1}C_d}{(u-d)\,{}^nSe^{R_f \frac{\tau}{N}}}
$$

American currency puts follow the same approach in which each node is evaluated

$$Max\lfloor 0, {}^nB + {}^nS\,{}^nD, K - {}^nS \rfloor$$

where

$$
{}^nB = \frac{u\,{}^{n+1}P_d - d\,{}^{n+1}P_u}{(u-d)e^{R_d \frac{\tau}{N}}}
$$

and

$$
{}^nD = \frac{{}^{n+1}P_u - {}^{n+1}P_d}{(u-d)\,{}^nSe^{R_f \frac{\tau}{N}}}
$$

and ${}^{n+1}P_u$ and ${}^{n+1}P_d$ are the values of the put nodes at jump $(n+1)$ for the up and down jumps, respectively, and all the other variables are defined the same as in the case of the call option. The term $(K - {}^nS)$ is the sufficient condition for early exercise.

The Binomial Model for European Currency Options

As was mentioned earlier, the binomial model also works for European options. The only modification is that early exercise need not be considered. For a European option, however, a shortcut exists with which to derive the option's value directly from the final set of nodes and their associated binomial probabilities of occurrence. This approach invokes the risk-neutrality argument of Cox and Ross that was presented in the development of the BSM model. The value of the European call is

$$C_0 = e^{-R_d \tau} \sum C_N p_N$$

where the C_N terms are the potential values at expiration and p_N are their risk-neutral probabilities of occurrence. This equation represents C_0 as the present value of the risk-neutral expected value of the payoff matrix at the final set of nodes. The assumption that spot exchange rates follow a multiplicative binomial process defines the probability of occurrence of each potential value at expiration. In the generalized case, the probability of an up move, denoted as p, is equal to

$$p = \frac{e^{(R_d - R_f)\frac{\tau}{N}} - d}{(u - d)}$$

Each potential cash flow at maturity has a number of paths. For example, with $N = 4$, the payoff that results from any combination of one up move and three down moves could be achieved with four possible paths (namely, *uddd*, *dudd*, *ddud*, and *dddu*). If j is defined as the number of up moves, then there are exactly

$$\frac{N!}{j!(N - j)!}$$

paths to any one expiration value, and the probability of any one path materializing is

$$p^j (1 - p)^{N-j}$$

The present value of the risk-neutral expected value of the terminal cash flows is then

$$e^{-R_d\tau} \sum \frac{N!}{j!(N-j)!} p^j (1-p)^{N-j} Max[0, u^j d^{N-j} S_0 - K]$$

This equation completes the European binomial model, but it is usually transformed into its more recognizable form by defining the variable a as the minimum number of up moves that would be required to make the option finish in-the-money so that

$$Max\lfloor 0, u^j d^{N-j} S_0 - K \rfloor = 0, \quad \text{for} \quad j < a$$

$$Max[0, u^j d^{N-j} S_0 - K] = u^j d^{N-j} S_0 - K, \quad \text{for} \quad j \geq a$$

then

$$C_0 = e^{-R_f\tau} S Z(a; N; p') - e^{-R_d\tau} K Z(a; N; p)$$

where Z is the cumulative density function of the binomial distribution and

$$p' = u e^{-(R_d - R_f)\frac{\tau}{N}} p$$

It is important to note that as N is allowed to grow large, the binomial distribution converges at the limit on the lognormal distribution. Therefore, one can say that with a sufficiently large number N of binomial paths, the binomial solution for European options will closely approximate the BSM value for a European option.

American Currency Options by Approximation

Several methods of valuing an American currency option by *analytic approximation* have appeared in the literature. The interest in these methods is that they achieve some degree of computational efficiency over the binomial model.

The finite difference method of Schwartz (1977); Parkinson (1977); Brennan and Schwartz (1977); and Brennan, Courtadon, and Subrahmanyam (1985) partitions the spot price of the underlying assets, here being foreign exchange, and the time to expiration into a fine grid that represents every possible time path.

Quadratic Approximation Method

A second method originates with the *compound option model* that dates back to Geske (1979) and Geske and Johnson (1984). Barone-Adesi and Whaley (1987) report that the compound option method is considerably quicker than the finite difference method, but it has the disadvantage that it requires evaluation of the cumulative bivariate and trivariate density functions.

   Barone-Adesi and Whaley (1987) propose a *quadratic approximation method* based on earlier work by MacMillan (1986). Similar to Jorion and Stoughton (1989a, 1989b), Barone-Adesi and Whaley define the early-exercise premium on an American option as the difference between the value of an American option and that of a similarly specified European option. For a call option, this premium, denoted e_c, is defined as

$$C' - C$$

where C' and C are the values of the American and European options, respectively. The key insight of the quadratic model is that the exercise premium must also obey the Black-Scholes partial differential equation. In other words, the quadratic approach treats the American exercise feature itself as an option. Hence it must obey the same partial differential equation.

Partial Differential Equation for Early-Exercise Premium

$$\frac{1}{2}\sigma^2 S^2 \frac{\partial^2 e_c}{\partial S^2} - R_d e_c + (R_d - R_f)S\frac{\partial e_c}{\partial S} - \frac{\partial e_c}{\partial \tau} = 0$$

If the early-exercise privilege has value, then there must exist a critical spot exchange rate, S^*, at which early exercise becomes optimal. S^* is a function of time to expiration as well as volatility and the domestic and foreign interest rates, as noted earlier. The value of an American call for values $S > S^*$ would be equal to

$$C' = [S - K], \quad S \geq S^*$$

For values of $S < S^*$, the quadratic approximation of the American call is

$$C' = C + A_2 \left(\frac{S}{S^*}\right)^{q_2}, \quad S < S^*$$

where

$$A_2 = \frac{S^*}{q_2}\left[1 - e^{-R_f \tau} N\left(d_1(S^*)\right)\right]$$

$$q_2 = \frac{1}{2}\left[-(N-1) + \sqrt{(N-1)^2 + 4\frac{M}{B}}\right]$$

$$N = 2\frac{(R_d - R_f)}{\sigma^2}$$

$$M = 2\frac{R_d}{\sigma^2}$$

$$B = 1 - e^{-R_d \tau}$$

$$d_1(s^*) = \frac{\ln\frac{S^*}{K} + \left(R_d - R_f + \frac{1}{2}\sigma^2\right)\tau}{\sigma\sqrt{\tau}}$$

where $N(*)$ is the cumulative normal density function.

All of the preceding variables are directly knowable except S^*, the critical spot rate that triggers early exercise. Barone-Adesi and Whaley provide an algorithm that iteratively converges on S^* within a tolerable level for error. Fortunately, once S^* for one strike has been estimated, it is not necessary to repeat the iterative procedure for similar options that differ only in terms of strike. This is because there is a linear relationship between critical S^*'s and strikes within a class of options:

$$S_2^* = \frac{S^*}{K}K_2$$

where S^*_2 and K_2 are the critical spot rate and strike, respectively, for another option with otherwise similar specifications.

For American put options, the quadratic approximation is

$$P' = P + A_1 \left(\frac{S}{S^{**}}\right)^{q_1} \quad \text{for} \quad S > S^{**}$$

$$P' = K - S \quad \text{for} \quad S \le S^{**}$$

where it is optimal to exercise the option at or below spot rate S^{**} and where

$$A_1 = -\frac{S^{**}}{q_1} \left[1 - e^{-R_f \tau} N\left(-d_1(S^{**})\right)\right]$$

$$q_1 = \frac{1}{2} \left[-(N-1) - \sqrt{(N-1)^2 + 4\frac{M}{B}}\right]$$

and N, M, B, d_1, and $N(*)$ are defined the same as in the procedure for the American call. Also,

$$S_2^{**} = \frac{S^{**}}{K} K_2$$

for a second put with everything the same except for strike.

Double Exercise Method

A third approach for approximating the value of an American currency option was developed by Ho, Stapleton, and Subrahmanyam (HSS) (1994). HSS estimate the value of an American option by combining the values of (a) a European exercise option and (b) a twice-exercisable option. The latter is a compound option that can be exercised either at the midpoint of its life or at normal expiration time.

The valuation of options that can be exercised only on a given number of dates goes back to work by Geske and Johnson (1984). In the Geske and Johnson framework, a European option has one given date when exercise is permitted. An American option has an infinite number of exercise dates because it is continuously exercisable. HSS produce an exponential relationship between the value of an American option and the number of exercise points allowed up to option expiration. This relationship allows them to estimate the value of an American option as

$$\ln \hat{C}' = \ln C_2' + (\ln C_2' - \ln C)$$

where $\hat{C}'$ is the estimated value of the American option, C_2' is the value of the twice-exercisable option, and C is the value of the European option. The same formula works for put options. The value of the twice-exercisable (i.e., double exercise) option comes from Geske and Johnson (1994) and works as follows:

$$C_2' = \lambda(K w_2 - S w_1)$$

where

$$w_1 = e^{-R_f \tau_1} N_1(-\lambda d_1') + e^{-R_f \tau_2} N_2(\lambda d_1', -\lambda d_1'', -\rho)$$

$$w_2 = e^{-R_d \tau_1} N_1(-\lambda d_2') + e^{-R_d \tau_2} N_2(\lambda d_2', -\lambda d_2'', -\rho)$$

where $\lambda = 1$ for a put option and $\lambda = -1$ for a call option, τ_1 is the time remaining until the first allowed exercise, τ_2 is the time until expiration, N_1 is the cumulative univariate normal distribution, and N_2 is the cumulative bivariate normal distribution. The remaining parameters are defined as

$$d_1' = \frac{\ln\left(\frac{S}{S_1^*}\right) + \left(R_d - R_f + \frac{1}{2}\sigma^2\right)\tau_1}{\sigma\sqrt{\tau_1}}$$

$$d_1'' = \frac{\ln\left(\frac{S}{K}\right) + \left(R_d - R_f + \frac{1}{2}\sigma^2\right)\tau_2}{\sigma\sqrt{\tau_2}}$$

$$d_2' = d_1' - \sigma\sqrt{\tau_1}$$

$$d_2'' = d_1'' - \sigma\sqrt{\tau_2}$$

$$\rho = \sqrt{\frac{\tau_1}{\tau_2}}$$

HSS provide an efficient iterative method for estimating the critical price S^*_1.

Method of First Passage

Yet another approach to American exercise valuation, proposed by Bunch and Johnson (1999), is based on the first passage of the critical price for optimal early exercise. Bunch and Johnson write about an American exercise put on shares of common stock, but the approach is readily generalized to American currency options.

Bunch and Johnson write the American put price as an integral involving the first-passage probability of the underlying stock price hitting the critical stock price level. The assumption is that the American put option will be exercised when the critical stock price level is hit. This makes the put price equal to the expectation of the discounted value of the exercise price minus the critical stock price, or

$$P = \underset{S_c}{Max} = \int_0^T e^{-R_d t}(K - S_c)f\,dt, \quad (S > S_c)$$

where S_c is the critical stock price. The first term on the right-hand side is the discount factor, the second is the payoff when exercise occurs, and the third term, f, is the first-passage probability, meaning the probability that the stock price will decline from S to S_c for the first time at time t.

Bunch and Johnson provide an exact calculation of S_c using a formula from Kim (1990) and noting that when $S = S_c$, the put has no time decay:

$$\frac{\partial P}{\partial \tau} = 0$$

This is because when the stock price declines to the critical price, it doesn't matter how much time is left to expiration. Alternatively, Bunch and Johnson describe this condition as where "the interest rate effect is exactly offset by the volatility effect." A direct implication of the Bunch and Johnson paper is that exercise of in-the-money puts should increase dramatically as maturity nears.

Chapter 8

Currency Futures Options

A currency futures option exercises into a currency futures contract, whereupon the in-the-money spread between the strike and the futures price becomes an immediate credit or debit to accounts having long and short positions.

The practical aspects of trading currency futures options were covered in Chapter 3. In this chapter, we will begin with a discussion on the relationship between futures, spot, and forward prices. Next, we will cover parity theorems for European and American currency futures options. Afterward, models for the valuation of futures options will be presented.

Currency Futures and Their Relationship to Spot and Forward Exchange Rates

The Forward Outright

Spot foreign exchange deals are agreements to promptly exchange sums of currencies. The *forward foreign exchange* rate applies to agreements for the exchange of sums of currencies at a date later than the spot value date.

The interest parity forward exchange rate is equal to

$$F = Se^{(R_d - R_f)\tau}$$

where F is a forward exchange rate, called the *outright*; S is the spot exchange rate; R_d is the domestic currency interest rate; R_f is the foreign currency interest rate; and τ is the time remaining to settlement. All exchange rates are assumed to be American quotation style (i.e., U.S. dollars per one unit of foreign exchange).

Forward points are defined as the difference between the outright and the spot exchange rate:

$$F - S = S(e^{(R_d - R_f)\tau} - 1)$$

Forward Contracts

A *currency forward contract* is an agreement between two counter-parties to exchange currencies at a fixed rate, called the *delivery price*, on a settlement or value day sometime in the future beyond the spot value date. In most instances, forward contracts are negotiated at delivery prices equal to the prevailing forward exchange rate; the initial value of such a forward contract is zero. Thereafter, the value of the contract assumes positive or negative values as a function of exchange rates, domestic and foreign interest rates, and the passage of time. On settlement day, T, the value of a forward contract to buy one unit of foreign exchange, denoted as V_T, is equal to

$$V_T = S_T - F_0$$

where F_0 is the delivery price that was established when the parties entered into the contract and S_T is the spot rate at settlement.

To exit a forward contract, one must do a second closing transaction. A closing transaction can be done at any time before the forward contract's value day. It forms the basis of how to value a forward contract. The closing transaction must settle on the same value date as the original forward transaction. The closing transaction for a forward contract to buy foreign currency consists of a second forward contract to sell foreign currency. The closing transaction for a forward contract to sell foreign currency consists of a second forward contract to buy foreign currency. There will be a residual cash flow at the forward value date representing the profit or loss on the forward transaction. The net present value of this residual amount is the value of the forward contract at any time before expiration.

Suppose that on day t, when time $\tau = (T - t)$ remains until the forward value date, we wish to value an existing forward contract to buy one unit of foreign exchange. The forward contract and the contract to close it have the following cash flows in domestic and foreign currency at value date T:

	Domestic currency	Foreign currency
Forward contract	$-F_0$	$+1$
Closing contract	$+F_t$	-1
Total	$F_t - F_0$	0

where F_0 is the original outright from when the forward contract was struck and F_t is the outright of the closing contract. The net present value of $F_t - F_0$ is the value of the forward contract at time t:

$$V_t = e^{-R_d \tau}(F_t - F_0) = e^{-R_f \tau} S_t - F_0 e^{-R_d \tau}$$

Currency Futures Contracts

A *currency futures contract* is different from a forward contract because profits and losses are settled between parties and the exchange Clearing House on a daily basis—that is, futures contracts are *marked-to-market* each business day on the basis of daily price movement.

On expiration day T, the futures price is expected to converge on the spot exchange rate:

$$f_T = S_T$$

Before expiration, the difference between the futures price and the spot exchange rate

$$f_t - S_t$$

is defined as the futures basis. The mark-to-market process, called *variation margin*, resets the value of the futures contract to zero each day.

The nature of the interest rate at which variation margin can be invested or borrowed is the focus in the theoretical distinction between futures and forward contracts. In the simplest case, it can be assumed that the interest rate is known with perfect certainty, meaning that it is nonstochastic. Cox, Ingersoll, and Ross (1981), building on earlier work by Black (1976), demonstrate that the futures price must equal the forward exchange rate if this assumption holds. Another way to express this is to say that if the interest rate is known with perfect certainty, the futures price, like the forward exchange rate, must obey the interest parity theorem. This will make the futures basis equal to the forward points.

Cox, Ingersoll, and Ross's proof of this theorem demonstrates that a rolling series of futures contracts can perfectly duplicate a forward contract, at least in the nonstochastic interest rate case. Their argument introduces the concept of a rollover futures hedge.

In a rollover futures hedge, the number of futures contracts is adjusted each day as a function of the known interest rate and the remaining time to expiration. The number of contracts is equal to

$$e^{-R_d(T-t)} = e^{-R_d \tau}$$

At time $t = 0$, the hedge would consist of $e^{-R_d T}$ contracts because T is the time remaining to expiration. The next day, an incremental amount of contracts must be added, to reflect the passage of one day. Finally, there would be one whole contract at expiration when $t = T$ and $e^{-R_d(0)} = 1$.

The following explanation of the Cox, Ingersoll, and Ross proof paraphrases Stoll and Whaley (1986) and Whaley (1986). Consider two portfolios, A and B. Portfolio A consists of a long forward contract negotiated at time $t = 0$ at the prevailing forward outright F_0 (quoted American style) to receive one unit of foreign exchange on day T, plus a long position in riskless domestic currency zero coupon bonds that mature on day T. The bonds have maturity value equal to F_0 worth of domestic currency; their initial present value is equal to

$$F_0 e^{-R_d T}$$

On day T, when the bonds mature and the forward contract settles, Portfolio A will be worth the spot exchange rate S_T. This is because the forward contract will be worth

$$(S_T - F_0)$$

and the bonds will mature to pay an amount equal to F_0.

Portfolio B consists of a rollover futures position that also expires on day T plus a long position in riskless domestic currency zero coupon bonds that mature on day T. The initial futures price is denoted as f_0. A sufficient amount of bonds are purchased to make their maturity value equal to f_0. The present value of the bonds is equal to

$$f_0 e^{-R_d T}$$

The daily mark-to-market of the rollover program is invested or financed at the domestic interest rate R_d. The value of Portfolio B on expiration day T will be equal to S_T. This is because the profit or loss on the

$$e^{-R_d(T-t)}$$

futures contracts will be marked-to-market each day in an amount equal to

$$e^{-R_d(T-t)}(f_t - f_{t-1})$$

where f_t is the futures price at the end of trading on day t and f_{t-1} is the futures price from the previous day. The future value of this amount on day T will be equal to

$$e^{R_d(T-t)}e^{-R_d(T-t)}(f_t - f_{t-1}) = (f_t - f_{t-1})$$

and the sum of all the future values of the daily mark-to-market will be equal to

$$f_1 - f_0$$

plus $\qquad f_2 - f_1$

plus $\qquad \ldots$

plus $\qquad \underline{S_T - f_{T-1}}$

which will equal $\qquad S_T - f_0$

assuming that the futures price at expiration f_T converges on the spot rate S_T. The value of portfolio B is equal to S_T, which is the sum of the values of the rollover hedge $(S_T - f_0)$ and the zero coupon bonds (f_0). Under the no-arbitrage rule, Cox, Ingersoll, and Ross conclude that the futures price f_0 must equal the forward exchange rate F_0 because the value of portfolio A is equal to the value of portfolio B.

Cox, Ingersoll, and Ross also speak to the case of stochastic interest rates, based on a discovery by Margrabe (1976). Margrabe's insight is that uncertainty about the interest rate is immaterial to the market, meaning that it would not count as market-priced risk unless it was correlated with the underlying spot exchange rate.

According to Margrabe, futures could have either a risk premium or a risk discount relative to the forward exchange rate, depending on the existence and sign of any correlation. As an empirical matter, studies by Cornell and Reinganum (1981) and Chang and Chang (1990) find no statistically significant difference between prices of currency futures and forwards. Moreover, Cornell and Reinganum also find no significant level of correlation between exchange rates and interest rates, a fact that is consistent with their other finding that currency futures in their sample have no risk premium or discount, in the Margrabe sense.

Arbitrage and Parity Theorems for Currency Futures Options

Several arbitrage and parity theorems for currency options were discussed in Chapter 4. Similar relationships also exist for futures options.

Currency Futures Options Have Nonnegative Prices

Futures options have nonnegative prices because the holder of the option is never obligated to exercise. This can be expressed as

European Currency Futures Options

$$C^f \geq 0; \quad P^f \geq 0$$

American Currency Futures Options

$$C^{f'} \geq 0; \quad P^{f'} \geq 0$$

where the superscript f denotes a futures option and the prime superscript denotes American exercise.

Properties of American Currency Futures Options

a. The value of an in-the-money American futures option is worth at least as much as its immediate exercise profit. The no-arbitrage condition implies the following inequalities:

$$C^{f'} \geq f_t - K$$
$$P^{f'} \geq K - f_t$$

b. The value of an American futures option is a positive function of the time remaining until expiration, all other things remaining equal:

$$C^{f'}(T - t_0) \geq C^{f'}(T - t_1)$$

$$P^{f'}(T - t_0) \geq P^{f'}(T - t_1)$$

where $t_1 > t_0$. An extension of the exercise date cannot diminish the value of an American futures option because immediate exercise is allowed at any time before expiration. This proposition is usually but not always true for European futures options.

c. American exercise options are never worth less than equivalent European exercise options:

$$C^{f'} \geq C^{f}$$

$$P^{f'} \geq P^{f}$$

This follows simply from the fact that early exercise is a privilege but not an obligation for the holder of the American exercise futures option.

The Relationship between European Currency Futures Options and Options on Actual Foreign Exchange

By definition, a European currency futures option can be exercised only on expiration day.

If the underlying futures contract also expires on option expiration day, and if it can be assumed that the futures price will converge on the spot rate at expiration, then there will be no difference at any point in time between the price of the European futures option and a European option on actual foreign currency:

$$C = C^{f}$$

$$P = P^{f}$$

where C and P are European options on actual foreign exchange and C^f and P^f are European futures options. This result does not hold when the futures expiration differs from the futures option's expiration.

Assume that the interest parity theorem strictly holds for futures prices

$$f = Se^{(R_d - R_f)\tau}$$

Then the lower boundaries for call and put options on actual foreign exchange that were presented in Chapter 4

$$C \geq Se^{-R_f \tau} - Ke^{-R_d \tau}$$
$$P \geq Ke^{-R_d \tau} - Se^{-R_f \tau}$$

can be translated into lower boundaries for currency futures options as

$$C^f \geq (f - K)e^{-R_d \tau}$$
$$P^f \geq (K - f)e^{-R_d \tau}$$

The Relationship between American Currency Futures Options and Options on Actual Foreign Exchange

For American futures options, the comparison to options on actual foreign exchange is less straightforward. For options with the same strike and expiration, the relative valuation depends on whether the foreign currency is at *discount* ($R_d < R_f$) or at *premium* ($R_d > R_f$). For a discount currency, the futures price must be less than the spot exchange rate. Hence an American futures call must be less valuable and an American futures put more valuable than corresponding American options on actual foreign exchange:

Discount Currencies

$$C^{f'} \leq C'$$
$$P^{f'} \geq P'$$

For a premium currency, the futures price must be greater than the spot exchange rate, which implies that an American futures call must be more valuable and an American futures put must be less valuable than corresponding American options on actual foreign exchange:

Premium Currencies

$$C^{f'} \geq C'$$

$$P^{f'} \leq P'$$

Put-Call Parity for European Currency Futures Options

Stoll and Whaley (1986) provide a put-call parity theorem for generalized futures options that is adaptable to European currency futures options. For a put and call struck at level K and with time τ remaining until expiration, the relationship is

Put-Call Parity for European Currency Futures Options

$$C^f - P^f = (f - K)e^{-R_d\tau}$$

Stoll and Whaley's proof of this relationship constructs a portfolio that consists of four parts:

1. A long currency futures rollover program that consists of a position in futures equal to $e^{-R_d\tau}$ that is adjusted each day
2. A long European futures put
3. A short European futures call
4. A long position in a riskless zero coupon domestic currency bond that matures on expiration day with value equal to $(f_0 - K)$

where f_0 is the futures price that prevails in the market at the start of the arbitrage program. Stoll and Whaley demonstrate that the value of this portfolio is zero on expiration day regardless of the level of the futures price.

Position	Initial cost of construction	Expiration values $S_T < K$	$S_T > K$
1. Rollover futures	0	$S_T - f_0$	$S_T - f_0$
2. Long put	$-P^f$	$K - S_T$	0
3. Short call	$+C^f$	0	$-(S_T - K)$
4. Long bonds	$-(f_0 - K)e^{-R_d\tau}$	$(f_0 - K)$	$(f_0 - K)$
Total	$C^f - P^f - (f_0 - K)e^{-R_d\tau}$	0	0

Under the no-arbitrage condition, the value must also be zero at all times before expiration, which proves the parity theorem.

Put-Call Parity for American Currency Futures Options

Stoll and Whaley's work can also be adapted to provide a put-call parity theorem for American currency futures options. As in the case of American currency options on spot exchange, put-call parity takes the form of an inequality. For an American futures put and futures call struck at level K and with a common expiration date T, the relationship is:

Put-Call Parity for American Currency Futures Options

$$f e^{-R_d\tau} - K \leq C^{f'} - P^{f'} \leq f - K e^{-R_d\tau}$$

The proof involves constructing one arbitrage portfolio for the left-hand side, called the *lower boundary*, and another arbitrage portfolio for the right-hand side, called the *upper boundary*. Because the futures puts and futures calls are American exercise, there is the possibility that either arbitrage portfolio might experience assignment of exercise at some point in time before expiration that we will denote as t^*.

The lower boundary arbitrage portfolio (Exhibit 8.1) consists of the following:

1. A long position in an American currency futures call with strike equal to K and expiration at time T. The initial cost equals $C^{f'}$. At some intermediate time, t^*, the option is worth

			Expiration value	
Position[1]	Initial value	Intermediate value	$S_T < K$	$S_T \geq K$
Long call	$-C^{f'}$	$+C_{t^*}^{f'}$	0	$(S_T - K)$
Short put	$+P^{f'}$	$-(K - f_{t^*})$	$-(K - S_T)$	0
Short rollover futures program[2]	0	$-(f_{t^*} - f_0)e^{-R_d(T-t^*)}$	$-(S_T - f_0)$	$-(S_T - f_0)$
Short bonds	$(f_0 e^{-R_d T} - K)$	$-(f_0 e^{-R_d(T-t^*)} - Ke^{R_d t^*})$	$-(f_0 - Ke^{R_d T})$	$-(f_0 - Ke^{R_d T})$
Total	$-(C^{f'} - P^{f'}) +$ $(f_0 e^{-R_d T} - K)$	$C^{f'} + K(e^{-R_d t^*} - 1) +$ $f_{t^*}(1 - e^{-R_d(T-t^*)}) > 0$	$K(e^{R_d T} - 1) > 0$	$K(e^{R_d T} - 1) > 0$

Lower boundary: $f_e^{R_d T} - K \leq C^{f'} - P^{f'}$

1. The position consists of a long call, short put, a short position in a rollover futures program, and an initial borrowing of $(f_0 e^{-R_d T} - K)$ dollars.

2. The short rollover futures program consists of a short position in $e^{-R_d(T-t^*)}$ contracts with daily rebalancing.

Exhibit 8.1 Put-call parity for American currency futures options.

$Cf't*$. At expiration, the futures price is assumed to converge on the spot exchange rate, and the option is worth

$$C^{f'}_T = MAX[0, S_T - K]$$

2. A short position in an American currency futures put with strike equal to K and expiration at time T. The initial proceeds of the sale equal Pf'. At some intermediate time, t^*, the option might be exercised, whereupon the portfolio would be debited the difference between the strike and the current futures price

$$-(K - f_{t^*})$$

Technically, the arbitrage portfolio also receives delivery of one futures contract, which would have no instantaneous value.

3. A short rollover futures program that takes a position of $e^{-R_d(T-t)}$ contracts with daily adjustment. On expiration day, the portfolio is short one contract (because $t = T$ on that day). At expiration, this program will have value equal to

$$-(S_T - f_0)$$

4. A short position in bonds (i.e., borrowed funds) with initial value equal to

$$(f_0 e^{-R_d T} - K)$$

and value at maturity (i.e., repayment) on expiration day equal to

$$-(f_0 - K e^{+R_d T})$$

The proof is given by the fact that the value of the arbitrage portfolio is always positive, both at expiration and in the intermediate case. At expiration, the value of the arbitrage portfolio is equal to

$$K(e^{R_d T} - 1)$$

which is positive as long as the interest rate is greater than zero. In the intermediate case, we assume involuntary exercise of the short put against the arbitrage portfolio; Exhibit 8.1 shows that the intermediate value of the arbitrage portfolio is also positive. Because both the intermediate value and expiration value are positive, the no-arbitrage rule requires that the initial cost of the portfolio

$$(f_0 e^{-R_d T} - K) - (C^{f'} - P^{f'})$$

must be positive, which completes the proof.

The proof of the upper boundary condition (Exhibit 8.2) runs along similar lines, except that the rollover futures program is always long $e^{R_d(T-t)}$ contracts.

Black's Model for European Currency Futures Options

This section develops a model for European futures options.

As was described earlier, where the futures option and its underlying futures contract share a common expiration date, the value of the futures option should be the same as an option on physical foreign exchange. This is because the futures option has no intermediate cash flows associated with owning it beyond the payment of the premium and because the futures price ought to converge on the spot exchange rate at expiration.

In the general case, futures options have shorter lives than their associated deliverable futures contracts. For example, a futures contract that expires in October delivers a December futures contract. This is why a special model for European futures options is needed.

Black (1976) adapted the Black-Scholes common stock option–pricing model to work on a generic class of European commodity futures options. What follows is a presentation of the Black model as applied to currency futures options.

Assumptions for Black's Model

Black's European futures option model requires three assumptions:

			Expiration value	
	Upper boundary: $C^{f'} - P^{f'} \leq f - Ke^{-R_dT}$			
Position[1]	Initial value	Intermediate value	$S_T < K$	$S_T \geq K$
Short call	$+C^{f'}$	$-(f_{t^*} - K)$	0	$-(S_T - K)$
Long put	$-P^{f'}$	$+P^{f'}$	$(K - S_T)$	0
Long rollover futures program[2]	0	$(f_{t^*} - f_0)e^{+R_dt^*}$	$(S_T - f_0)e^{R_dT}$	$(S_T - f_0)e^{R_dT}$
Long bonds	$-(f_0 - Ke^{-R_dT})$	$(f_0e^{R_dt^*} - Ke^{-R_d(T-t^*)})$	$(f_0e^{R_dT} - K)$	$f_0(e^{R_dT} - K)$
Total	$(C^{f'} - P^{f'}) - (f_0 - Ke^{-R_dT})$	$P^{f'}_{t^*} + f_{t^*}(e^{-R_dt^*} - 1)$ $+ K(1 - e^{-R_d(T-t^*)}) > 0$	$S_T(e^{R_dT} - 1) > 0$	$S_T(e^{R_dT} - 1) > 0$

1. The position consists of a short call, a long put, a long position in a rollover futures program, and an investment in bonds with initial value $(f_0 - Ke^{-R_dT})$ dollars.

2. The long rollover futures program consists of a long position in $e^{+R_d(T-t^*)}$ contracts with daily rebalancing.

Exhibit 8.2 Put-call parity for American currency futures options.

1. There are no taxes, no transaction costs, and no restrictions on taking long or short positions in futures options or futures contracts. All transactors are price takers.
2. The domestic interest rate is riskless and constant over the future option's life.
3. Instantaneous changes in the futures price are generated by a diffusion process of the form

$$\frac{df}{f} = \alpha\, dt + \sigma\, dz$$

where α is the drift term, dt is an instant in time, σ is the standard deviation of the process, and dz is a stochastic variable that is independent across time and is normally distributed with zero mean and standard deviation equal to the square root of dt.

Under these assumptions, it is possible to construct a local hedge for a long position in a currency futures call option using a short position in some number of currency futures contracts. As is common in financial theory, the rate of return on the hedged position is assumed to be no more and no less than the risk-free interest rate R_d.

Given the assumptions, the price of a futures call must conform to the following partial differential equation:

Black's Partial Differential Equation for Currency Futures Options

$$R_d C^f - \frac{1}{2}\sigma^2 f^2 \frac{\partial^2 C^f}{\partial f^2} - \frac{\partial c^f}{\partial \tau} = 0$$

The boundary conditions for the value of European futures calls and puts at expiration are given as

$$C_T^f = Max[0,\, f_T - K]$$

$$P_T^f = Max[0,\, K - f_T]$$

This means that at expiration, the value of either futures option is the greater of zero and the amount by which the option is in-the-money.

Black produces a model for European futures options by solving the partial differential equation subject to the expiration boundary conditions:

Black's European Currency Futures Option Model

$$C^f = e^{-R_d\tau}\left[fN(h) - KN(h - \sigma\sqrt{\tau})\right]$$

$$P^f = e^{-R_d\tau}\left[-f\left(N(-h)\right) + K\left(N(-h + \sigma\sqrt{\tau})\right)\right]$$

where

$$h = \frac{\ln\left(\frac{f}{K}\right) + \frac{\sigma^2}{2}\tau}{\sigma\sqrt{\tau}}$$

It is interesting to note that the foreign currency interest rate does not explicitly appear in the Black futures option model, although it does factor into the futures-spot relationship. In a sense, the currency futures option model is blind with respect to the fact that what underlies the futures contract is foreign exchange; it might as well be a stock market index or an agricultural commodity for all that the model is concerned. All that matters is the form of the stochastic process that drives the futures price, that the domestic currency interest rate is riskless and constant, and that it is possible to operate the local hedge risklessly between futures and futures options.

Exhibit 8.3 contains the partial derivatives for Black's model. Exhibit 8.4 shows a numerical example for futures puts and calls on the Japanese yen.

The Valuation of American Currency Futures Options

Comments on Optimal Early Exercise

American futures options can be optimally exercised before expiration if they are sufficiently in-the-money to compensate for the possibility that were they left alive, they might pick up even more intrinsic value.

Currency futures calls

$$\delta_{call} \equiv \frac{\partial C^f}{\partial f} = e^{-R_d \tau} N(h)$$

$$\gamma_{call} \equiv \frac{\partial^2 C^f}{\partial f^2} = \frac{e^{-R_d \tau} N'(h)}{f \sigma \sqrt{\tau}}$$

$$\theta_{call} \equiv \frac{\partial C^f}{\partial \tau} = -R_d f e^{-R_d \tau} N(h) + R_d K e^{-R_d \tau} N(h - \sigma \sqrt{\tau}) + f e^{-R_d \tau} N'(h) \frac{\sigma}{2\sqrt{\tau}}$$

$$\kappa_{call} \equiv \frac{\partial C^f}{\partial \sigma} = e^{-R_d \tau} f \sqrt{\tau} N'(h)$$

$$\rho_{call} \equiv \frac{\partial C^f}{\partial R_d} = -\tau C^f$$

Currency futures puts

$$\delta_{put} \equiv \frac{\partial P^f}{\partial f} = -e^{-R_d \tau} N(-h)$$

$$\gamma_{put} \equiv \frac{\partial^2 P^f}{\partial f^2} = \frac{e^{-R_d \tau} N'(h)}{f \sigma \sqrt{\tau}}$$

$$\theta_{put} \equiv \frac{\partial P^f}{\partial \tau} = R_d f e^{-R_d \tau} N(-h) - R_d K e^{-R_d \tau} N(-(h - \sigma \sqrt{\tau})) + f e^{-R_d \tau} N'(h) \frac{\sigma}{2\sqrt{\tau}}$$

$$\kappa_{put} \equiv \frac{\partial P^f}{\partial \sigma} = e^{-R_d \tau} f \sqrt{\tau} N'(h)$$

$$\rho_{put} \equiv \frac{\partial P^f}{\partial R_d} = -\tau P^f$$

Exhibit 8.3   Partial derivatives for Black's futures option model.

Whaley (1986) points out that the Black model reveals that the lower bound for a deep-in-the-money European futures call is equal to

$$(f - K)e^{-R_d \tau}$$

Parameters		
Futures price	84.01	
Strike	84.00	
Days	71	
Volatility	17.45%	
Interest rate	4.70%	
Output	*Call*	*Put*
Price	2.560	2.550
Delta	0.511	(0.480)
Gamma	0.061	0.061
Theta	0.018	0.018
Vega	0.146	0.146
Rho	0.079	(0.083)

Note: Vega has been scaled down by 1/100 and theta by 1/365.

Exhibit 8.4 Numerical example of Black's European futures options model—Japanese yen futures.

This is because both of the terms $N(h)$ and $N(h + \sigma \sqrt{\tau})$ in the Black model approach unity as the futures price rises above the strike. For the American futures option, however, the intrinsic value

$$(f - K)$$

can be realized at any time. This forms the lower bound for the option. Because the term $e^{-R_d \tau}$ is less than one ($R_d > 0$), the lower bound for the in-the-money American futures option must be greater than the lower bound of a similar European futures option. This is because

$$(f - K) > (f - K)e^{-R_d \tau}$$

Therefore, early exercise of an American futures option could be theoretically optimal.

At some sufficiently high futures price, denoted as f^*, the value of the American call will be equal to its intrinsic value, whereupon the holder of the option will be indifferent to its early exercise (Exhibit 8.5).

For values of f less than f^*, the value of early exercise, written as epsilon, is equal to the difference between the values of the American and European futures options:

$$\varepsilon = C^{f'} - C^f \quad \text{for} \quad f < f^*$$

where $C^{f'}$ is an American futures call and C^f is a similarly specified European futures call.

At futures prices above f^* the value of epsilon is given by the difference between the intrinsic value of the American call and the value of the European call:

$$\varepsilon = (f - K) - C^{f'} \quad \text{for} \quad f \geq f^*$$

As f grows very large compared to the strike, the European call approaches its lower bound, equal to the present value of its intrinsic value,

$$(f - K)e^{-R_d T}$$

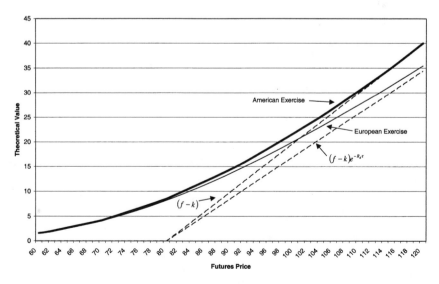

Exhibit 8.5   American and European calls on the yen.

This term represents the interest income that could be earned on investing the proceeds from early exercise.

The Binomial Model

Hull (1997) shows that the binomial option-pricing model can be adapted with little modification to work on American futures options. As in the case of Black's European futures option model, the binomial approach is blind to the fact that it is foreign currency that underlies the futures contract. In other words, the binomial model for American currency futures options is the same model that would be appropriate for other types of futures options.

Hull's approach is to model an American futures option in a similar way as would work for an American option on a dividend-paying common stock. The only modification is that the domestic interest rate is made to stand in for the dividend rate. The resultant model is not substantially different from the binomial model described in Chapter 7. But the up-and-down jump terms and the probability term p (the probability of an upward jump) need to be redefined as

$$u = e^{\sigma \sqrt{\frac{\tau}{N}}}$$

$$d = e^{-\sigma \sqrt{\frac{\tau}{N}}}$$

$$p = \frac{1 - d}{u - d}$$

The Quadratic Approximation Method

Whaley (1986) adapted the Barone-Adesi and Whaley quadratic approximation method to handle American futures options. The model is

$$C^{f'} = C^f + A_2 \left(\frac{f}{f^*} \right)^{q_2}, \quad f < f^*$$

$$C^{f'} = f - K, \quad f \geq f^*$$

where

$$A_2 = \left(\frac{f^*}{q_2}\right)\left(1 - e^{-R_d\tau} N\left(d_1(f^*)\right)\right)$$

$$d_1(f^*) = \frac{\left(\ln\left(\frac{f^*}{K}\right) + \frac{1}{2}\sigma^2\tau\right)}{\sigma\sqrt{\tau}}$$

$$q_2 = \frac{(1 + \sqrt{1 + 4b})}{2}$$

$$b = \frac{2R_d}{\sigma^2(1 - e^{-R_d\tau})}$$

The value f^* can be found iteratively by solving

$$f^* - K = C^{f'}(f^*) + \left[1 - e^{-R_d\tau} N\left(d_1(f^*)\right)\right]\frac{f^*}{q_2}$$

For American futures puts, the quadratic model is

$$P^{f'} = P^f + A_1 \left(\frac{f}{f^{**}}\right)^{q_1}, \quad f > f^{**}$$

$$P^{f'} = K - f, \quad f \le f^{**}$$

$$A_1 = -\left(\frac{f^{**}}{q_1}\right)\left(1 - e^{-R_d\tau} N\left(-d_1(f^{**})\right)\right)$$

$$q_1 = \frac{(1 - \sqrt{1 + 4b})}{2}$$

where f^{**} is the optimal exercise futures price for the American futures put and all other terms are defined as in the formulation for the American futures call. The value of f^{**} can be found iteratively by solving

$$K - f^{**} = P^{f'}(f^{**}) - \left[1 - e^{-R_f\tau} N\left(-d_1(f^{**})\right)\right]\frac{f^{**}}{q_1}$$

Alternatively, the value of an American futures option can be approximated using the Ho, Stapleton, and Subrahmanyam approach discussed in Chapter 7 by setting the foreign interest rate (R_f) equal to the domestic interest rate (R_d). The intuition for this is that a futures option is analogous to an option on an asset that pays a yield equal to the risk-free rate of interest, meaning that it has no cost of carry.

Chapter **9**

Barrier Currency Options

An *exotic currency option* is an option that has at least one nonstandard feature to set it apart from ordinary vanilla puts and calls. Presently, exotic currency options are traded exclusively in the interbank market. Exotic currency options are mainly European exercise.

All of the major foreign exchange banks deal in exotic currency options. Some exotic currency options have become such standard fare with traders and hedgers that it is an exaggeration to call them exotic.

The most popular variety of exotic option is the *barrier option,* which is the topic of this chapter. Barrier options go out of existence or come into existence when the market spot exchange rate trades at or through some predetermined barrier level.

Throughout this chapter it is assumed that the barrier is continuously monitored. This is never literally true because foreign exchange markets are closed over weekends and at other times. However, the foreign exchange market comes the closest among all markets to fulfilling the condition in that trading takes place 24 hours a day on weekdays.[1]

In some markets, the holder of a barrier option receives a cash payment or rebate if the option is extinguished before expiration. As a rule, however, currency barrier options do not pay rebates.[2]

Barrier currency options are said to be *path-dependent* in that their value is affected by the entire history of the movement of the spot exchange rate throughout their lives. In contrast, vanilla currency options are not path-dependent because their value at expiration is determined solely by the final level of the spot exchange rate relative to the option strike. Intermediate values of the spot

---

1. See Berger 1996 for discussion of noncontinuous barrier monitoring.
2. See Haug 1998 for barrier options models that feature rebates.

exchange rate are irrelevant for the vanilla option but not for the barrier option, because the latter's existence is governed by the barrier all throughout its life.

Why all the interest in barrier options? Barrier options are highly leveraged directional trades that cost a fraction of the purchase price of a vanilla option. Barrier options have interesting volatility properties. For example, it is possible to construct a short-volatility trade with the purchase of barrier options. Being able to construct a fixed-premium short-volatility position using barrier options is an improvement over far riskier conventional short-volatility trades that require taking short positions in vanilla options. Hedgers too have found that some barrier currency options can be useful and cost-effective in managing currency risk.

This chapter looks at a handful of barrier options that have become important to traders and hedgers, specifically, single- and double-barrier options, binary barrier options, and contingent premium options.

Single-Barrier Currency Options

Taxonomy of Single-Barrier Options

A *knock-out barrier option* contains a cancellation feature that causes the option to extinguish when and if the spot exchange rate touches or trades through an out-strike barrier level. By definition, the out-strike for a knock option is located out-of-the-money. Suppose that dollar/yen is trading at 120. An example of a knock-out put is a USD call/JPY put that is struck at 120 and out-struck at 115. If dollar/yen trades at 115, this option immediately cancels. Otherwise, for as long as the 115 level does not trade, the knock-out functions the same as a vanilla option. Knock-out calls are called *down-and-out calls*; knock-out puts are called *up-and-out puts*.

A *knock-in barrier option* is an option that does not come into existence unless the spot exchange rate breaches a specified in-strike level. If the in-strike level trades, the knock-in permanently turns into a vanilla put or call. However, if the in-strike never trades during the option's life, the knock-in will expire worthless at expiration, even if it is in-the-money. The in-strike for a knock-in option is located out-of-the money. In the example in the previous paragraph, 115 would be a valid in-strike for a knock-in USD call/JPY put.

Kick-out and kick-in options are similar to knock-out and knock-in options except that the out-strike or in-strike is located in-the-money. An example of an up-and-out kick-out call would be a USD put/JPY call struck at 120 with an out-strike at 110. Similarly, a down-and-out kick-out put would be a USD call/JPY put struck at 120 with an out-strike at 125.

The combination of an in-option and an out-option with the same strike is equivalent to a vanilla option. This is true because when the barrier is triggered, the out-option extinguishes but the in-option springs to life. Therefore,

$$C_{out} + C_{in} = C$$

$$P_{out} + P_{in} = P$$

Knock Options

Haug (1998), following Rich (1994) and Reiner and Rubinstein (1991a), provides a convenient framework for valuing barrier calls and puts based on earlier work by Merton (1973) and Black and Cox (1976). Haug defines the following equations that will be used repeatedly in this chapter:

$$Z1 = \phi e^{-R_f \tau} S N(\phi x_1) - \phi e^{-R_d \tau} K N(\phi x_1 - \phi \sigma \sqrt{\tau})$$

$$Z2 = \phi e^{-R_f \tau} S N(\phi x_2) - \phi e^{-R_d \tau} K N(\phi x_2 - \phi \sigma \sqrt{\tau})$$

$$Z3 = \phi e^{-R_f \tau} S \left(\frac{H}{S}\right)^{2(\mu+1)} N(\eta y_1) - \phi e^{-R_d \tau} K \left(\frac{H}{S}\right)^{2\mu} N(\eta y_1 - \eta \sigma \sqrt{\tau})$$

$$Z4 = \phi e^{-R_f \tau} S \left(\frac{H}{S}\right)^{2(\mu+1)} N(\eta y_2) - \phi e^{-R_d \tau} K \left(\frac{H}{S}\right)^{2\mu} N(\eta y_2 - \eta \sigma \sqrt{\tau})$$

$$\mu = \frac{R_d - R_f - \frac{1}{2}\sigma^2}{\sigma^2}$$

The symbol H refers to the barrier; other terms are as were previously defined, and η and ϕ are index reference variables:

Knock-out Calls and Puts

$$C_{down\ \&\ out}(K > H) = Z1 - Z3,\ with\ \eta = 1\ and\ \phi = 1$$

$$P_{up\ \&\ out}(K < H) = Z1 - Z3,\ with\ \eta = -1\ and\ \phi = -1$$

Knock-in Calls and Puts

$$C_{down\ \&\ in}(K > H) = Z3,\ with\ \eta = 1\ and\ \phi = 1$$

$$P_{up\ \&\ in}(K < H) = Z3,\ with\ \eta = -1\ and\ \phi = -1$$

Why Knock-out Options Are Popular

Exhibit 9.1 shows the theoretical value of a knock-out USD put/JPY call for comparison to a vanilla option. The option strike is 120 and the barrier is 125. This exhibit demonstrates that the barrier option is smaller in value than the vanilla in the proximity of the barrier. The barrier option converges on the vanilla at progressively lower values of the spot exchange rate as the probability of the barrier being knocked out diminishes. This is reflected in the behavior of

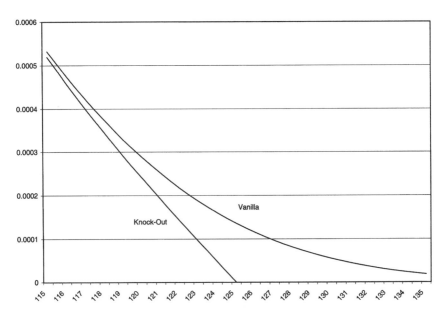

Exhibit 9.1 Knock-out USD Put/JPY call: strike = 120; out-strike = 125; 90 days; vol = 15%; R_d = 5%; R_f = 1%.

the delta relative to the delta of the vanilla (Exhibit 9.2). When the barrier is hit, the delta of the barrier option becomes instantly zero. The knock-out delta is considerably higher than the vanilla delta when spot is close to, but not equal to, the barrier.

This explains part of the popularity of knock-out puts and calls on foreign exchange. These options appeal to traders because they offer relatively low-cost, high-delta vehicles for placing speculative bets on currencies.

But knock-out options are also popular among hedgers, and legitimately so. Consider a Japanese exporter who is long dollars against yen at the 120 level. The knock-out USD put/JPY call might be cost-effective as a hedge because it affords the downside protection that the exporter is seeking. The fact that the option is knocked out at 125 may not be of great concern to the hedger because the value of his dollars would have appreciated by 5 yen by the time that the knock-out is extinguished.

However, it should be noted that the exporter would have to either buy a new knock-out option or devise a new hedging strategy were the 125-barrier to be broken. One simple way to stay continuously hedged through a barrier event would be to establish a

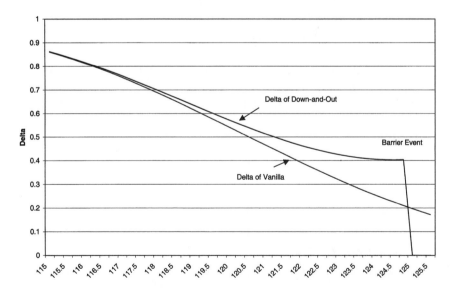

Exhibit 9.2 Deltas of down-and-out USD put/JPY call and vanilla USD put/JPY call: 30 days; vol = 15%; R_d = 5%; R_f = 1%; out-strike = 125; strike = 120.

stop-loss order to sell one-half of his dollars at the 125 barrier. If the barrier were subsequently triggered, the short dollar position would function as a short-run delta hedge in approximately the same way as an at-the-money-forward USD put/JPY call. Moreover, the short dollar position could be later exchanged with a dealer as part of a transaction to buy a vanilla USD put/JPY call.

Kick Options

By definition, the out-strike zone for the kick family of barrier options is where the option is in-the-money.

Kick-out Options

Consider a kick-out USD call/JPY put struck at 120 and out-struck at 125. The potential gains from owning a kick-out option are limited; in the example, the kick-out put could at best finish by something slightly less than 5 yen in-the-money. Accordingly, its price should be relatively small.

Following Haug (1998) and recognizing earlier work by Rich (1994) and Taleb (1997):

Kick-out Calls and Puts

$$C_{up\,\&\,out}(K < H) = Z1 - Z2 + Z3 - Z4, \text{ with } \eta = -1 \text{ and } \phi = 1$$

$$P_{down\,\&\,out}(K > H) = Z1 - Z2 + Z3 - Z4, \text{ with } \eta = 1 \text{ and } \phi = -1$$

Consider the following kick-out call:

Option	USD put/JPY call
Face	$10,000,000
Initial spot	120
Strike	120
Out-strike	115
Interest rate (USD)	5%
Interest rate (JPY)	1%
Volatility	15%
Term	30 days

This option has a theoretical value of only $31,567. Yet it has the potential value of nearly $434,782 (i.e., 5 yen of expiration value), which would be its maximum value were the spot exchange rate to come close to but never touch the 115 level. Exhibit 9.3 shows the value of this option at 30 days to expiration and 3 days to expiration compared to a 30-day vanilla call. With 30 days to expiration, the kick-out call has little or no delta, gamma, vega, or time decay. In effect, the option is caught between Scylla (meaning the strike) and Charybdis (the out-strike)—and being torn in opposite directions by the strike and out-strike crushes the option's sensitivity to movements in the spot exchange rate, time, and volatility.

A very different picture arises during the final days of the kick-out's life, as can be seen in Exhibit 9.3. The kick-out comes to life in a way that resembles the behavior of a butterfly spread near its expiration (as was discussed in Chapter 5). Exhibit 9.3 demonstrates that when only three days remain before expiration, the kick-out assumes its maximum value where spot is midway between the strike and the out-strike. Also note that the sign of the kick-out's delta changes somewhere in the region between the strike and out-strike.

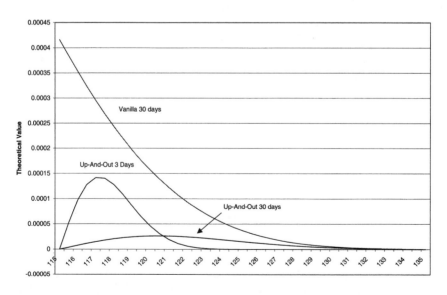

Exhibit 9.3 Kick-out up-and-out USD put/JPY call: out-strike = 115; vol = 15%; R_d = 5%; R_f = 1%.

Kick-out options are far less important to option end users than are knock-out options. Kick-outs are of limited use in hedging; they might even be called a hazard to a hedger because they extinguish in the region where the hedger needs protection the most.

A public debate on barrier options erupted in 1995 when some Japanese exporters reportedly attempted to hedge their long dollar/yen positions with kick-out USD put/JPY call options when dollar/yen was rapidly declining. Prominent hedge-fund manager George Soros publicly expressed displeasure with the concept of the kick-out structure. He blamed the sudden drop in the dollar below the level of 90 yen on panic selling of dollars by the exporters when their kick-out options extinguished. Whether or not one accepts Soros's analysis of the drop in the dollar (and this author does not), the episode highlights the dangers of hedging with kick-out options.

Kick-in Options

Kick-in options come to life only when the option is sufficiently in-the-money so as to trigger the in-strike. The relative cheapness of these options comes from the fact that there is a range of in-the-moneyness, between the strike and the in-strike, that cannot be captured at expiration unless the in-strike is triggered. Exhibit 9.4 compares the theoretical values of a 30-day kick-in USD call/JPY put struck at 120 and in-struck at 130 to a vanilla USD call/JPY put. Notice that the kick-in always has a positive delta but naturally lags the vanilla in accumulating value as spot rises. Once the in-strike is triggered, the kick-in mutates into a vanilla option.

Kick-in Calls and Puts

$$C_{up\ \&\ in}(K < H) = Z2 - Z3 + Z4,\ with\ \eta = -1\ and\ \phi = 1$$

$$P_{down\ \&\ in}(K > H) = Z2 - Z3 + Z4,\ with\ \eta = 1\ and\ \phi = -1$$

Kick-ins are useful to traders who anticipate a large directional move. Hedgers like them when they want to buy cheap insurance against a large move in an exchange rate. Rich (1994) and Taleb (1997) provide discussion of kick-in option valuation.

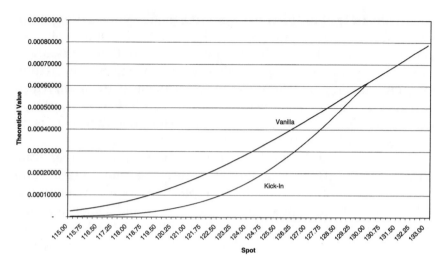

Exhibit 9.4 Kick-in USD call/JPY put: strike = 120; in-strike = 130; 30 days.

Static Replication of Barrier Options

Some insight can be gleaned about knock-out options from an artifact of option algebra called *put-call symmetry* (formally described by Carr 1994). For vanilla options, assuming constant and equal volatility across all strikes, put-call symmetry dictates that the following relationship must hold:

$$\frac{C}{\sqrt{K_C}} = \frac{P}{\sqrt{K_P}}$$

where

$$\sqrt{K_C K_P} = F$$

K_C and K_P refer to the strikes of the call and the put, respectively. The second equation is a condition that places the strikes of the call and the put equidistant from each other on opposite sides of the forward. One can think of put-call symmetry as saying that a call struck at twice the forward has the same value as a put struck at half the forward.

To illustrate, if the forward were 100, then a symmetrical pair of strikes for a call and a put would be 105 and 95.24, respectively. The symmetry principle says that the ratio of each of these option values to the square root of their strikes would have to be equal. However, one should note that unlike the put-call parity theorem, which is a true arbitrage relationship, put-call symmetry is merely an exercise in algebra conditioned on the assumption that there is no smile or skew in option volatility.

Carr, Ellis, and Gupta (1998) use put-call symmetry to replicate barrier options. Their basic model requires that the domestic and foreign interest rates be equal. The replication for a down-and-out call consists of a long position in a vanilla call and a short position in some number of units of a vanilla put that is struck symmetrically opposite to the call around the out-strike of the down-and-out call:

$$C_{D\&O} = C(K) - \sqrt{\frac{K}{K_P}} P(K_P)$$

where the put strike is defined as

$$K_P = \frac{H^2}{K}$$

Consider a down-and-out call with the following parameters:

Option	USD put/JPY call
Face	$10,000,000
Spot	120
Strike	115
Out-strike	123
Interest rate (USD)	5%
Interest rate (JPY)	5%
Volatility	15%
Term	6 months

This knock-out call is worth $124,711 (equal to .0001084 times the face in yen) according to the barrier option–pricing model that was presented earlier.

According to Carr, Ellis, and Gupta, the value of the knock-out call should be equal to the difference between a vanilla USD put/ JPY call and some number of symmetrically struck USD call/JPY put options. Using put-call symmetry, the strike of the yen put is 131.56 and the number of puts is 1.069. Using BSM—and assuming a constant volatility across all of these options—it can be shown that the value of the 115-strike yen call is $232,278 and the value of the 131.56-strike yen put is $100,571. Therefore:

	Units	Option value	Total
USD put/JPY call (115 strike)	1.00	$232,278	$232,278
Less			
USD call/JPY put (131.56)	1.06956	$100,571	($107,566)
Synthetic knock-out			$124,711

In the example, the symmetry replication appears to work. Bowie and Carr (1994) produce upper and lower bounds for knock-out options in the more general case in which the domestic and foreign interest rates are not equal. Yet the approach raises the question of whether vanilla options could be used to manufacture real-world knock-out options (and a whole host of other barrier options, as is suggested in the Carr, Ellis, and Gupta paper). The initial problem is that the 131.56 strike USD call/JPY put in the example, being a low-delta option, might have a very different quoted volatility than the 115-strike USD put/JPY call. This was assumed away in the theory because the notion of volatility smile and skew is nonexistent in put-call symmetry. Moreover, the replication technique requires that the vanilla put and call be liquidated if the knock-out barrier, 123, is struck. This might not be possible to accomplish at reasonable cost. The wind-down of the replication vanilla options requires the repurchase of 1.07 units of the 131.56-strike put and the sale of the 115-strike yen call. Either of these options could be skewed, meaning that the outcome of the whole exercise is uncertain from the beginning.

Aggravating the predicament of the replicator is the necessity to do as many as four vanilla option trades and hence cross as many as four option bid-ask spreads. Two trades are required to establish the replication portfolio and possibly two more to remove them if the barrier option is knocked out. These costs could present an insurmountable argument against static replication. Proponents of the technique point out that static replication requires no dynamic rebalancing and hence no need to do periodic spot trading to achieve delta equality with the barrier option. However, this exaggerates the advantage of static hedging. In the context of running a sizable option market–making operation, significant economies of scale in hedging exist because the book may contain positions that are naturally offsetting (being long some options and short others or having positions in both puts and calls).

Stopping Time

A subtle problem with put-call symmetry replication of barrier options concerns the concept of *stopping time*. Stopping time is the expected time of the first breach of the barrier.[3] It is an important theoretical concept that is ubiquitous today in discussions of the mathematics of barrier option–pricing models (see Levy 1948 and Taleb 1997).

Stopping time is an inverse function of volatility because increases in the latter imply that the expected time remaining to a barrier event will have grown shorter. Likewise, movements in the spot exchange rate can affect stopping time because the closer the spot rate is to a barrier, the shorter the expected time to the option being knocked out.

All of this raises an important question about barrier options, namely, what is the correct quoted volatility to apply to a barrier option when stopping time is shorter than time remaining to the expiration date? The answer is that the appropriate volatility for a barrier option is the point on the implied volatility surface that corresponds to the stopping time.

For example, if the spot exchange rate were close to the barrier, stopping time would be small, even if the expiration date were far away. It might be appropriate to use a short-dated volatility, maybe even as short as one week or one day, to price a barrier option that is close to being out-struck. However, if the spot exchange rate sub-

---

3. The concept of stopping time dates back at least as early as Levy (1948). See discussion in Taleb 1997.

sequently moved away from the barrier, stopping time would lengthen and the option volatility would have to be read further out on the implied volatility surface.

This presents a strong case against static replication of a barrier option using European vanilla options. The stopping time of a vanilla option experiences no dynamic evolution of volatility because it is always equal to the expiration date, regardless of where spot happens to be.

Stopping time poses the same problem when it comes to determining the term to maturity for the domestic and foreign interest rates that are ingredients in the valuation of a barrier option. Here the barrier problem resembles that of the American exercise vanilla option in that the latter has no defined stopping time because of the possibility of optimal early exercise.

Binomial and Trinomial Models

A considerable amount of work has been done on the use of the binomial model in the valuation of barrier options. One advantage of using a *lattice model* is that it can work on the odd barrier option that features American exercise. Direct application of the binomial model requires that each node of the tree be adjusted for the occurrence of a barrier event.

Unfortunately, the binomial approach has been shown to have serious biases when used for barrier options, even when the number of branches in the tree is large. Boyle and Lau (1994) show that substantial errors occur when a barrier is located between adjacent branches of the binomial tree. They suggest defining the partitioning of time so as to make the resulting tree branches as close as possible to the barrier.

Ritchken (1998) introduces a trinomial option model that is capable of valuing single- and double-barrier options. In the trinomial model, the spot exchange rate is constrained to move in one of three ways—up, middle, and down:

$$Up: \quad \lambda \sigma \sqrt{\Delta T}$$

$$Middle: \quad 0$$

$$Down: \quad -\lambda \sigma \sqrt{\Delta T}$$

where ΔT is a partitioned unit of time. The probabilities of up, middle, and down moves are given by

$$p_u = \frac{1}{2\lambda^2} + \frac{\mu\sqrt{\Delta T}}{2\lambda\sigma}$$

$$p_m = 1 - \frac{1}{\lambda^2}$$

$$p_d = \frac{1}{2\lambda^2} - \frac{\mu\sqrt{\Delta T}}{2\lambda\sigma}$$

where

$$\mu = R_d - R_f - \frac{\sigma}{2}$$

and λ is the parameter that controls the width of the gaps between the layers of the lattice. Ritchken's trick is to set λ so as to guarantee a barrier event after an integer number of successive moves. Ritchken reports impressive computational efficiency with his trinomial model for barrier options.

Yet the ultimate limitation with any classical binomial or trinomial approach is that the stopping time concept implies that each node in a lattice logically might have a volatility unique to itself.

More advanced tree models are presented in Dupire (1994), Derman and Kani (1994a, 1994b), and Rubinstein (1994). In the Derman and Kani approach, the entire volatility surface is integrated into a flexible, arbitrage-free binomial lattice. The advantage of being able to incorporate the strike skew and term structure of volatility into the lattice can amount to an important refinement in the pricing of barrier options. For example, one would expect that the presence of a significant strike skew in favor of the low delta options would allow a dealer to improve on the pricing of knock-out options. This could be seen from Carr's replication approach, where the value of a knock-out call is equal to a vanilla minus a number of out-of-the-money puts. The greater the strike skew, the more that can be earned from the sale of the puts; hence the lower the market price for the knock-out.

However, implied binomial tree models are obviously complex in application. Yet the approach does have merits for achieving an enhanced understanding of how the market prices barrier options. Chriss (1997) and Berger (1996) are good sources for further discussion of these new models.

Double-Barrier Knock-out Options

A *double-barrier option* knock-out option has two barriers, one that is in-the-money and another that is out-of-the-money. For example, at spot dollar/yen equal to 120, the double-barrier option might be struck at 120 and have two out-strikes, one at 110 and the other at 130.

The valuation of double knock options is problematic. Kunitomo and Ikeda (1992; also see Haug, 1998) provide this model for a double knock-out call option where the upper barrier is denoted as U and the lower barrier as L:

$$
\begin{aligned}
C_{double} = e^{-R_f \tau} S \sum_{n=-\infty}^{\infty} & \left[\left(\frac{U^n}{L^n} \right)^{\mu} [N(d_1) - N(d_2)] \right. \\
& \left. - \left(\frac{L^{n+1}}{U^n S} \right)^{\mu} [N(d_3) - N(d_4)] \right] \\
- e^{-R_d \tau} K \sum_{n=-\infty}^{\infty} & \left[\left(\frac{U^n}{L^n} \right)^{\mu-2} [N(d_1 - \sigma\sqrt{\tau}) - N(d_2 - \sigma\sqrt{\tau})] \right. \\
& \left. - \left(\frac{L^{n+1}}{U^n S} \right)^{\mu-2} [N(d_3 - \sigma\sqrt{\tau}) - N(d_4 - \sigma\sqrt{\tau})] \right]
\end{aligned}
$$

where

$$
d_1 = \frac{\ln\left(\frac{SU^{2n}}{KL^{2n}}\right) + \left(b + \frac{\sigma^2}{2}\right)\tau}{\sigma\sqrt{\tau}}
$$

$$
d_2 = \frac{\ln\left(\frac{SU^{2n}}{UL^{2n}}\right) + \left(b + \frac{\sigma^2}{2}\right)\tau}{\sigma\sqrt{\tau}}
$$

$$
d_3 = \frac{\ln\left(\frac{L^{2n+2}}{KSU^{2n}}\right) + \left(b + \frac{\sigma^2}{2}\right)\tau}{\sigma\sqrt{\tau}}
$$

$$
d_4 = \frac{\ln\left(\frac{L^{2n+2}}{SU^{2n+2}}\right) + \left(b + \frac{\sigma^2}{2}\right)\tau}{\sigma\sqrt{\tau}}
$$

$$
\mu = \frac{2b}{\sigma^2} + 1
$$

$$
b = R_d - R_f
$$

In practice, the infinite series terms converge rapidly, making it unnecessary to have to evaluate more than a few terms (you could restrict the range on n to go from -5 to $+5$, for example). Haug (1998) provides the companion model for double knock-out puts.

Exhibit 9.5 shows the valuation of a double knock-out USD put/JPY call at various levels of quoted volatility. The exhibit gives visual confirmation to the obvious fact that double knock-out options are short-volatility trades. In fact, stopping time for a double-barrier knock-out is likely to be very short, following from the fact that the option can be knocked out from either above or below.

Geman and Yor (1996) provide a mathematically sophisticated alternative to the Kunitomo and Ikeda formulation, based on excursions theory, that produces a Laplace transformation for double-barrier options. Ritchken's trinomial model also handles double-barrier options with some modification.

One of the most popular double-barrier trades is the *double knock-out straddle*. Purchasing a vanilla straddle (i.e., buying the same-strike put and call) is a long-volatility trade. The owner of the vanilla straddle is hoping that actual volatility will be enormous so

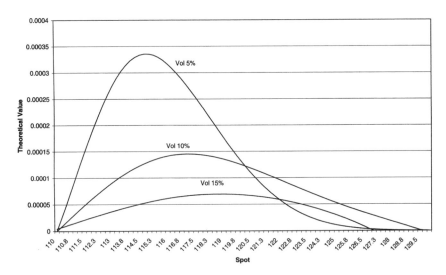

Exhibit 9.5   Double-barrier USD put/JPY call: 90 days; $S = 120$; $K = 120$; barriers at 110 and 130.

that either the put or the call will be driven deep-into-the money. The owner of a vanilla straddle is also better off if quoted volatility rises. The cost of maintaining a long position in a straddle is the decay in premium over time.

By the same logic, taking a short position in a vanilla straddle is a short-volatility trade. The writer of a vanilla straddle is hoping that the spot foreign exchange rate will stay right in place, making the straddle expire worthless. The writer benefits when quoted volatility drops because the straddle could be repurchased at a lower price. Along the way, the writer of the straddle collects time decay.

Things are totally reversed when a straddle is created with knock-out barriers. By market convention, breach of either barrier extinguishes both the put and the call that comprise straddle. The owner of the knock-out straddle is short volatility, in the sense of both actual volatility and quoted volatility. The owner hopes that actual volatility will be low and that the straddle is never knocked out. He would be pleased to see quoted volatility drop so that the market price of the knock-out straddle would rise. In what may seem somewhat counterintuitive at first, the owner of a knock-out straddle collects time decay; as time passes, the probability that the straddle will be knocked out drops and the structure becomes worth more.

Binary Barrier Options

A *binary option,* sometimes called a *digital option,* is defined to have a lump-sum payoff function. Binaries are quoted as the ratio of premium to payoff. For example, a binary quoted "3 to 1" means that the option buyer would receive three dollars, if the option expires in-the-money, for every one dollar in premium paid to the option writer.

European Binary Options

A *European exercise vanilla binary option* pays a lump sum of domestic currency at expiration provided the option is in-the-money. There are binary puts and binary calls. European binary options that pay one unit of domestic currency can be modeled as a fragment of the BSM model:

European Vanilla Binary Options

$$C_{Binary} = e^{-R_d \tau} N(x)$$

$$P_{Binary} = e^{-R_d \tau} \left(1 - N(x)\right)$$

A European vanilla binary option does not qualify as a barrier option. It is not path-dependent because the only condition for the option to pay is that it be in-the-money at expiration. What happens between the time that the option is dealt and when it expires is irrelevant.

One-Touch Binary Options

A *one-touch binary option* pays a lump sum of domestic currency provided that a specific in-strike trades during the life of the option. This option is sometimes called a *bet option*. For example, with spot dollar/yen trading at 120, the binary option could be structured to pay a sum of $1 million provided the spot level 130 trades at some time during the life of the option.

Reiner and Rubinstein (1991b) offer a model to value a single-barrier binary option that pays a lump sum W immediately after the barrier is hit:

One-Touch Binary Option

$$C_{OTB} = W \left[\left(\frac{H}{S}\right)^{a+b} N(\phi z) + \left(\frac{H}{S}\right)^{a-b} N(\phi z - 2\phi b \sigma \sqrt{\tau}) \right]$$

where

$$z = \frac{\ln\left(\frac{H}{S}\right)}{\sigma \sqrt{\tau}} + b\sigma \sqrt{\tau}$$

$$a = \frac{\mu}{\sigma^2}$$

$$b = \frac{\sqrt{\left(\mu + \left(2 \ln(1 + R_d)\right)\sigma^2\right)}}{\sigma^2}$$

$$\mu = \ln\left(\frac{1 + R_d}{1 + R_f}\right) - \frac{1}{2}\sigma^2$$

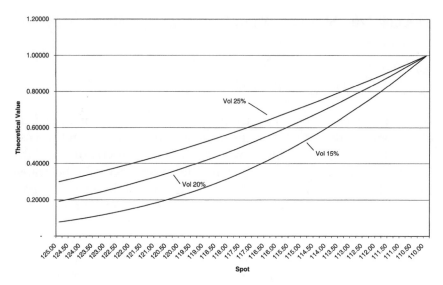

Exhibit 9.6 One-touch binary options: 90 days; barrier at 110.

where $\phi = 1$ for a put, meaning the option is *down and in ($S > H$)* and $\phi = -1$ for a call, meaning the option is *up and in ($S < H$)*. Exhibit 9.6 shows the theoretical valuation of a one-touch USD put/JPY call at differing levels of option volatility—the higher the volatility, the greater the value of the one-touch because the probability of the barrier being struck is higher.

Double-Barrier Binary Range Options

Perhaps the most interesting binary option is the *double-barrier binary range option*. This option has two barrier strikes, for example, 115 and 130, to continue with the running example of dollar/yen barrier options. The option is an *out* option because it is structured to pay a lump sum at expiration provided neither 115 nor 130 is struck during the life of the option.

Double-barrier binary range options are analytically the same thing as a *box trade* but with barriers. In a box trade, the trader who goes long the box buys both a call spread and a put spread so as to create a fixed payoff regardless of the location of the spot exchange rate at expiration. For example, a five-yen-wide box (Exhibit 9.7) could consist of the following four positions:

Long 120 USD call/JPY put
Short 125 USD call/JPY put
Long 125 USD put/JPY call
Short 120 USD put/JPY call

Boxes are essentially financing devices. The buyer of a box is in effect lending the present value of the width of the box, in this case 5 yen, to the writer of the box. *Vanilla boxes* are creatures of the listed option markets. The box in the example could be transformed into a double-barrier binary range option by inserting barriers at 115 and 130. This structure is unique to the interbank option market.

Double-barrier binary range options are popular with traders who want to express short-volatility views without being short vanilla options. The most common vanilla trade to express short-volatility views is the sale of a straddle. The danger with a short straddle trade is that the writer creates an exposure to negative gamma. Negative gamma implies that the option writer is at risk to whipsaw moves in the spot exchange rate that could theoretically

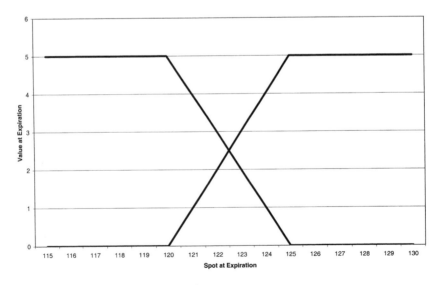

Exhibit 9.7 USD/JPY 120–125 box.

expose the option writer to extreme risk. What is alluring about the double-barrier binary range option is that a trader can get into a short-volatility trade by paying a fixed premium.

Hui (1996) develops the theoretical value for a double-barrier binary range option in a Black-Scholes environment:

Double-Barrier Binary Range Option

$$C_{DBB} = \sum_{n=1}^{\infty} \frac{2\pi n W}{L^2} \left[\frac{\left(\frac{S}{H_1}\right)^{\alpha} - (-1)^n \left(\frac{S}{H_2}\right)^{\alpha}}{\alpha^2 + \left(\frac{n\pi}{L}\right)^2} \right]$$

$$\times \sin\left(\frac{n\pi}{L} \ln \frac{S}{H_1} \right) e^{-.5\left[(n\pi/L)^2 - \beta \right] \sigma^2 \tau}$$

for $H_2 > H_1$, the payoff is W, and where

$$L = \ln\left(\frac{H_2}{H_1} \right)$$

$$\alpha = -\frac{1}{2}(k_1 - 1)$$

$$\beta = -\frac{1}{4}(k_1 - 1)^2 - \frac{2R_d}{\sigma^2}$$

$$k_1 = 2(R_d - R_f)/\sigma^2$$

Hui establishes that his equation, though exact in its valuation of the double-barrier binary, contains a convergent series that can be well approximated by evaluating only a few terms.

Exhibits 9.8 and 9.9 demonstrate that the double-barrier binary is short volatility and benefits from the passage of time. Note that the option depicted in these exhibits pays one dollar if neither of the barriers is struck; accordingly, the theoretical value can be interpreted as the premium expressed as the percentage of the payoff.

There are also double-barrier binary range options that are *in* options, meaning that they pay the binary payoff provided that either of the barriers is hit during the life of the option. This is a long-volatility strategy because the owner of the option is counting on a sufficiently large move in the spot exchange rate to cause either barrier to be struck.

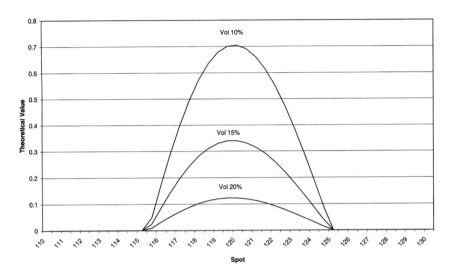

Exhibit 9.8   Double-barrier binary range options at various implied volatilities; barriers at 115 and 125; 30 days.

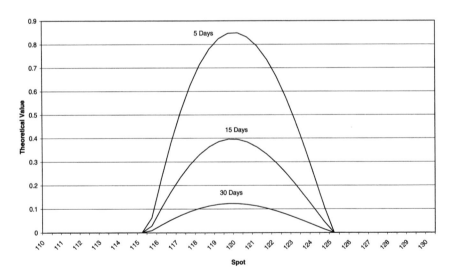

Exhibit 9.9   Double-barrier binary range options at various terms to expiration; barriers at 115 and 125; 30, 15, and 5 days.

Contingent Premium Options

A *contingent premium option* is an option that requires its owner to pay no premium up front. However, if certain premium strikes are hit during the life of the option, the option holder must immediately pay money to the writer of the option. For example, the holder of the option could get a "free" USD call/JPY put struck at 120. However, if 115 trades, the option holder would be obligated to pay a one-time premium equal to 1 percent of the option face. There could be a second premium strike as well, such as 110, which when traded would require the holder to pay an additional 1 percent premium.

Contingent premium options are easy to manufacture. In the example cited in the previous paragraph, an option dealer is swapping a vanilla option to his customer in exchange for a package of one-touch options that represent the contingent premiums for the vanilla option.

Consider the following example. Suppose that a trader wished to purchase a USD call/JPY put as specified by:

USD Call/JPY Put

Face	$10,000,000
Spot	120
Strike	120
Expiry	90 days
Volatility	15%
Interest rate (USD)	5%
Interest rate (JPY)	1%
Value (% face)	2.485%

Instead of paying cash for the option, the customer might be willing to assign to the dealer two one-touch options, one struck at 117 and the other at 115. Each one-touch would require a payment equal to 1.898 percent of the vanilla's face, which can be deduced from the fact that the 117 and 115 one-touch options are worth .737 and .572, respectively, per dollar of payoff. In the worst case, if dollar/yen hits both the 117 and 115 barriers, the customer will be obligated to pay a total of 3.80 percent of the vanilla face. On the other hand, if the dollar stays above 117, the customer will have succeeded in acquiring the vanilla option without making a cash outlay.

Contingent premium options are a useful substitute for the directional risk-reversal trade that many bank proprietary traders are fond of doing. As was described in Chapter 5, traders sometimes express a directional view, which, for example, could be bullish, by buying a 25-delta call and selling a 25-delta put. This trade can be established for zero or close-to-zero premium. Everything is wonderful if the spot exchange rate goes up, as predicted. But when the trade goes wrong, meaning that the spot rate goes down, the trader is left with an active, short gamma position in the form of the short put option. The outcome from trying to hedge the short put is indeterminate. Here is where the contingent premium might be preferable, because the worst thing that can materialize with this exotic option is that the trader has to pay some option premium.

What the Formulas Don't Reveal

All varieties of barrier options critically depend on knowing whether a barrier has been struck, and herein lies one of the most contentious issues in derivatives. Industry practice is to have the option-dealing bank assume the role of barrier-determination agent, despite the obvious conflict of interest.

Complicating the arrangement is the fact that foreign exchange transaction prices are not readily observable, except to the actual counterparties. Foreign exchange transactions are private conversations between two parties; no public record of trades exists as it does in the listed equity markets. Then there is the question of what constitutes a legitimate barrier event in terms of the defining trade. For example, it is logical that a transaction of de minimis size should not constitute a barrier event. Trading in thin markets is another problem—for example, trading done during the early Monday morning hours in Australia and New Zealand might not be counted. For some exchange rates, there is the question of whether a barrier event could be inferred from a cross rate—in other words, could a euro/yen option be knocked by implying a barrier event from the euro/dollar and dollar/yen exchange rates? Not surprisingly, a number of disputes have arisen between barrier counterparties, some of which have led to lawsuits.

A subtle conflict of interest exists between the writer and the holder of barrier options. Consider the case of the knock-out USD put /JPY call having its strike at 115 and its out-strike at 123 when dollar/yen is trading at 115. The dealer of this option, like all dealers, would wish to maintain delta neutrality. Consequently, the dealer's hedge would consist of a dynamic short dollar/yen spot position. If the spot exchange rate were to move upward, in the direction of the out-strike, the dealer would be obliged to remove a portion of the short dollar/yen hedge by buying dollars. If the option were knocked out at 123, the dealer would want to remove the balance of the short dollar position that was serving as the hedge as fast as possible. But in fact, dealers sometimes liquidate their hedges in anticipation that the spot exchange rate will subsequently breach the barrier. For example, suppose that dollar/yen is well bid at 122.80. If the dealer feels 123.00 or higher levels are imminent, she will not wait to buy the dollars to totally remove the hedge. The conflict is that this transaction, referred to as an *anticipatory de-hedging transaction,* may materially raise the probability that the barrier will be struck.[4]

Many times dealers execute de-hedging orders through the use of stop-loss orders. The execution of such an order automatically knocks out the barrier option and at the same time removes any residual spot position from the dealer's hedging book. Spot traders will attest to the fact that the behavior of the underlying spot market reflects the presence of these de-hedging stop orders, some of which are quite large.

Readers should not be left with the impression that barrier options are hopelessly biased in favor of market makers. In fact, barrier options present considerable risk to dealers because these options sometimes introduce insurmountable hedging problems (see Taleb 1997).

---

4. See Hsu 1997.

Chapter 10

Nonbarrier Exotic Currency Options

Nonbarrier currency options are used more by hedgers than by currency traders. There is a great variety of nonbarrier currency options, but the focus in this chapter will be on the options that are common in the marketplace. Those are *average rate options, compound currency options, basket options,* and *quantos options.*

Average Rate and Average Strike Currency Options

Average options, also called *Asian options,* exist in the foreign exchange market but are more prevalent in physical commodities markets.

Average options are useful when a commodity or asset is susceptible to price manipulation. An average option makes it more difficult for either the buyer or the writer of the option to be cheated because a series of prices during the averaging period would have to be rigged to materially disadvantage someone. Average options are also useful in situations where a hedger is primarily concerned with the average price of a commodity or currency of which he must make regular purchases or sales.

Intuitively, one would expect that an average option would have to be less valuable than a vanilla option. This is because the standard deviation of an average of a series of prices that is not perfectly autocorrelated has to be less than the standard deviation of a single price in the series. In other words, average options should sell for smaller implied volatilities than vanilla options (Kemna and Vorst 1990).

There are two types of average options: the *average rate* (sometimes called *average price)* and the *average strike* option. As their names suggest, the average rate option is in- or out-of-the-money at expiration, depending on where the option's strike is relative to the average observed price over the averaging period. The payoff functions for average rate calls and puts are defined as

Average Rate Call
$$Max[0, A - K]$$

Average Rate Put
$$Max[0, K - A]$$

where A represents the average rate and K represents the option strike price.

In the case of an average strike option, the strike is an average calculated from observed spot exchange rates. This means that the strike is actually not known until the end of the averaging period, which usually corresponds to the option's expiration. The payoff functions of average strike options are defined as

Average Strike Call
$$Max[0, S_T - A]$$

Average Strike Put
$$Max[0, A - S_T]$$

The average might be calculated from observations that span the option's entire life or from observations taken from a shorter period ending with the option's expiration day.

For either type of average option, the average is usually taken to be the arithmetic average, but other averages, such as the geometric mean, are sometimes used. The choice of the mathematical form of the average turns out to be of importance to the modeling of average options. To get to the point, a closed-form solution for the geometric mean average option does exist, but there is no such solution for arithmetic mean options.

Geometric Mean Average Options

The geometric mean of a series of discrete observations on the spot exchange rate is given by

$$G = \left(\prod_{i=1}^{n} S_i\right)^{\frac{1}{n}}$$

Kemna and Vorst (1990) derive a closed-form solution for a continuous geometric mean call option on a non-dividend-paying stock. Ruttiens (1990) presents the Kemna and Vorst model for geometric mean average currency calls:

Geometric Mean Average Rate Currency Call

$$C^{gmaro} = e^{-R_d\tau} e^{d^*} S N(d_1) - e^{-R_d\tau} K N(d_2)$$

where

$$d_1 = \frac{\left[\ln\left(\frac{S}{K}\right) + \frac{1}{2}\left(R_d - R_f + \frac{1}{6}\sigma^2\right)\tau\right]}{\sigma\sqrt{\frac{\tau}{3}}}$$

$$d^* = \frac{1}{2}\left(R_d - R_f - \frac{1}{6}\sigma^2\right)\tau$$

$$d_2 = d_1 - \sigma\sqrt{\frac{\tau}{3}}$$

The reason that this closed-form solution exists is because the geometric mean itself must be lognormally distributed if the underlying time series of random variables is lognormally distributed. This convenient property does not hold for the arithmetic mean.

In the Kemna and Vorst formulation, the option is assumed to be at the beginning of its life and the averaging process is conducted over the entire life of the option. Unfortunately, the approach is not able to revalue a geometric option after the averaging period has already begun.

Arithmetic Mean Average Options

As mentioned, no closed-form solution exists for arithmetic mean options under the standard assumption that spot exchange rates follow a lognormal diffusion process.

Kemna and Vorst (1990) propose an efficient control variate Monte Carlo simulation strategy for arithmetic mean options. In their control variate approach, the value of the geometric mean counterpart option, whose value is known from the closed-form solution, is used as a lower bound to the arithmetic mean call option. Because the geometric mean of any series is never greater than the arithmetic mean, the geometric mean average call establishes a lower bound for the arithmetic mean call.

A different approach was taken by Levy (1990 and 1992), who developed an analytical closed-form solution that proves to be reasonably precise. Levy's approach is appealing because it accurately values arithmetic mean options without requiring the computational burden of Monte Carlo simulation. Levy's model is as follows:

Levy's Arithmetic Mean Currency Call

$$C^{amaro} = S_A N(d_1) - e^{R_d \tau} K N(d_2)$$

where

$$S_A = e^{-R_d \tau} \frac{t}{T} S_{AV} + \frac{S}{Tg}(e^{-R_f \tau} - e^{-R_d \tau})$$

$$d_1 = \frac{1}{\sqrt{V}} \left(\frac{1}{2} \ln D - \ln K \right)$$

$$d_2 = d_1 - \sqrt{V}$$

$$V = \ln D - 2(R_d \tau + \ln S_A)$$

$$D = \frac{1}{T^2} \left[M + (t S_{AV})^2 + \frac{2t S S_{AV}}{g}(e^{g\tau} - 1) \right]$$

$$M = \frac{2S^2}{g + \sigma^2} \left[\frac{e^{(2g+\sigma^2)\tau} - 1}{(2g + \sigma^2)} - \frac{(e^{g\tau} - 1)}{g} \right]$$

$$g = (R_d - R_f)$$

In Levy's formulation, time starts at $t = 0$ and runs to expiration time T; time remaining to expiration, τ, is equal to $(T - t)$. The term S_{AV} represents the arithmetic average of the known spot rates. All other terms are as previously defined.

To arrive at the value of an arithmetic put, Levy suggests the following parity relationship:

Put-Call Parity for Arithmetic Mean Options

$$C_{amaro} - P_{amaro} = S_A - e^{-R_d \tau} K$$

Turnbull and Wakeman (1991) also provide approximation formulas for average rate options.

Compound Currency Options

A *compound option* is an option that delivers another option upon exercise. A *ca-call* is a call option that delivers a vanilla call upon expiration. A *ca-put* is a call option that delivers a vanilla put upon exercise. There are also put options that deliver vanilla calls and puts. Compound options were briefly mentioned in Chapter 7 as being the foundation of the Barone-Adesi and Whaley quadratic approximation model for American currency options.

Geske (1979) develops a model to value an option on a share of common stock as a compound option. His motivation stems from a theoretical concept from corporation finance that a share of stock can be thought of as itself an option. In this paradigm, the firm in its totality consists of a series of claims to future cash flows. The ownership of the firm is divided into two classes. Bondholders have priority on the firm's cash flow up to some maximum level. A simple way to model the bonds is to think of them as zero coupon bonds. The common stock then becomes an option consisting of the right, but not the obligation, to purchase the entire firm from the bondholders for a strike price equal to the maturity value of the firm's debt. Declaration of bankruptcy would amount to the shareholders' allowing their option to expire unexercised in a state of being out-of-the-money. If one were to assume that the total value of the firm (i.e., the combined value of all the shares of the stock and all the bonds) were to follow a diffusion process plus all the other standard option-pricing theory assumptions, then the value of the common stock would be given by the Black-Scholes model. But the value of an option on a share of stock would be an entirely different matter. It would be an option on an option. Also, the share of stock could not follow a diffusion process because it is an option on an asset, namely the firm, which is assumed to follow a diffusion process.

Insofar as currency options are concerned, compound options naturally exist because there is a demand for such options.

Compound options require the definition of some new variables: Let τ be the time to expiration of the underlying *daughter* vanilla option and τ^* be the time to expiration of the *mother* compound option. K_c is the strike of the compound option.

To keep things compact, define the binary variables ϕ and η such that

Call on a call	$\phi = 1$ and $\eta = 1$
Call on a put	$\phi = 1$ and $\eta = -1$
Put on a call	$\phi = -1$ and $\eta = 1$
Put on a put	$\phi = -1$ and $\eta = -1$

The compound options under discussion are European exercise. At the time of expiration, T^*, the holder of the compound option has the right but not the obligation to exercise. Exercise of a compound call requires payment of the strike K_c to receive a vanilla currency call or put. Exercise of a compound put requires the delivery of a vanilla call or put in exchange for the strike K_c. This can be expressed as

Compound Option on Vanilla Call at Expiration

$$O_T^{compound} = MAX\big[0, \phi\big[C(S_{T*}, K, T - T^*, \eta) - K_c\big]\big]$$

Compound options obey a put-call parity theorem:

Compound Option Put-Call Parity

$$O^{compound}(\phi = 1) - O^{compound}(\phi = -1) = \eta\big[C(S, \tau^*, \eta) - K_c\big]e^{-R_d\tau^*}$$

The first terms on the left-hand side of the equation are a compound call and compound put. The value of the vanilla call ($\eta = 1$) or put ($\eta = -1$) priced at compound expiration is represented by $C(S, \tau^*, \eta)$.

Following Geske (1979) and Briys (1998), the value of a compound option on a vanilla call or put on one unit of foreign exchange is given by the following:

Compound Currency Option

$$O^{compound} = \phi\eta e^{-R_f \tau^*} S N_2(\phi\eta x, \eta y, \phi\rho)$$

$$- \phi\eta e^{-R_d \tau} K N_2(\phi\eta x - \phi\eta\sigma\sqrt{\tau}, \eta y - \eta\sigma\sqrt{\tau^*}, \phi\rho)$$

$$- \phi K_c e^{-R_d \tau} N(\phi\eta x - \phi\eta\sigma\sqrt{\tau})$$

where

$$\rho = \sqrt{\frac{\tau}{\tau^*}}$$

$$x = \frac{\ln\left(\frac{e^{-R_f \tau} S}{e^{-R_d \tau} S_{cr}}\right)}{\sigma\sqrt{\tau}} + \frac{1}{2}\sigma\sqrt{\tau}$$

$$y = \frac{\ln\left(\frac{e^{-R_f \tau^*} S}{e^{-R_d \tau^*} K}\right)}{\sigma\sqrt{\tau}} + \frac{1}{2}\sigma\sqrt{\tau^*}$$

N_2 [a,b,ρ] is the cumulative bivariate normal distribution that covers the portion from minus infinity to a and from minus infinity to b and where ρ is the correlation coefficient. The value S_{cr} can be found by iteration of following equation:

$$\eta S_{cr} e^{-R_f(\tau^*-\tau)} N(z) - \eta K e^{-R_d(\tau^*-\tau)} N\left(z - \sigma\sqrt{\tau^* - \tau}\right) - K_c = 0$$

where

$$z = \frac{\ln\left(\frac{e^{-R_f(\tau^*-\tau)} S_{cr}}{e^{-R_d(\tau^*-\tau)} K}\right)}{\sigma\sqrt{\tau^* - \tau}} + \frac{1}{2}\sigma\sqrt{\tau^* - \tau}$$

The tricky aspect to trading compound options is the selection of the compound strike. Obviously, the higher the strike on the compound option, the more it costs to "buy" the vanilla through exercise of the compound option, and hence the smaller the initial value of the compound option. Yet a hedger must also balance the cost of the compound option against an alternative strategy of buying a vanilla option (with expiration at time T) that could be sold at the time of the compound option expiration if the option is not needed.

Basket Options

A *basket currency option* is a put or a call on a collection of currencies taken together as a portfolio. By definition, a basket option is all-or-none exercise, meaning that there is no allowance for partial exercise of some of the currencies in the basket. Basket options can be cash or physically settled.

European basket options can be valued with the BSM model, but the user must have an estimate of the implied volatility of the basket of currencies. This can be derived from the implied volatilities of each of the currencies with respect to the base currency, which are called the *leg volatilities*, as well as from the implied volatilities of each of the associated cross exchange rates, which are called the *cross volatilities*. There are a total of $N(N + 1)/2$ such terms for a basket that is comprised of N currencies. There are N leg volatilities and $N(N - 1)/2$ cross volatilities.

Consider the example of a basket composed of euros, pounds, and yen where the base currency is the dollar. Necessary to calculate the basket's implied volatility are the implieds for the legs, USD/JPY, EUR/USD, and GBP/USD plus the implieds for the crosses GBP/EUR, GBP/JPY, and EUR/JPY. It is possible to derive a set of implied correlations from these volatilities. The implied correlation between currencies 1 and 2 is given by

$$\rho_{1,2} = \frac{\sigma_1^2 + \sigma_2^2 - \sigma_{1/2}^2}{2\sigma_1\sigma_2}$$

where σ_1^2 and σ_2^2 are the variances of exchange rates 1 and 2, and $\sigma_{1/2}^2$ is the variance of the cross rate of exchange between currencies 1 and 2. For example, the correlation between euro/dollar and dollar/yen is given by

$$\rho(EUR/USD, USD/JPY) = \frac{\sigma^2_{\frac{EUR}{USD}} + \sigma^2_{\frac{USD}{JPY}} - \sigma^2_{\frac{EUR}{JPY}}}{2\sigma_{\frac{EUR}{USD}}\sigma_{\frac{USD}{JPY}}}$$

The implied correlations can be used to create a set of covariance terms:

$$COV(1, 2) \equiv \sigma_{12} = \rho_{12}\sigma_1\sigma_2$$

that completes the variance-covariance matrix, V

$$V = \begin{bmatrix} \sigma_1^2 & \sigma_{12} & \sigma_{13} \\ \sigma_{21} & \sigma_2^2 & \sigma_{23} \\ \sigma_{31} & \sigma_{32} & \sigma_3^2 \end{bmatrix}$$

The implied variance of the basket is equal to the variance-covariance matrix premultiplied by the row vector of the currency weights and postmultiplied by the column vector of the currency weights. The weight of each currency is defined as its percentage component in the basket. The implied volatility of the basket is equal to the square root of the implied variance. The value of a European basket option can be found directly from the forward exchange rate version of the BSM model, discussed in Chapter 4. DeRosa (1996) contains a detailed numerical example of the pricing of a basket option.

Portfolio managers and corporate treasurers favor basket options. Motivation comes from savings of option premium with the basket option by comparison to the cost of purchasing a strip of options, one for each separate currency. This savings results from the fact that the implied volatility of the basket is less than the average of the separate currency implied volatilities (see Hsu 1995).

Said another way, the value of the basket option must be less than the value of a strip of vanilla currency options because there is a possibility that the basket option might expire out-of-the-money, whereas one or more of the options in the strip might expire in-the-money. The principle can be understood in terms of correlation. Imagine a trader buying a basket option and simultaneously selling a strip of vanilla options on the component currencies in the basket. The net premium would be positive, as has been said. The combination would be *long correlation*. Conversely, the combination of being short the basket and long the strip would be *short correlation*, because the strip is more valuable when the correlation between the basket components breaks down.

Quantos Options

A *quantos option* is an option on a foreign stock index that features an implied fixed exchange rate. This option gives its holder the equivalent of having an option on a foreign stock index, such as the Nikkei, that is denominated in an alternative currency, such as the U.S. dollar. The value of a quantos option is dependent on the level of the foreign stock index but not on the exchange rate.

The payoff function of quantos calls and puts at expiration time T is given by

$$C_T^{quantos} = Max[\bar{S}Z_T - \bar{S}K, 0]$$

$$P_T^{quantos} = Max[\bar{S}K - \bar{S}Z_T, 0]$$

where $\bar{S}$ is the fixed level of the exchange rate and Z is the foreign stock index.

Derman, Karasinski, and Wecker (1990) and Dravid, Richardson, and Sun (1993) solve for the value of the European quantos options:

Quantos Options

$$C_t^{quantos} = \left[Z_t e^{(R_f - D')\tau} N(d_1) - K N(d_2)\right]\bar{S}e^{-R_d\tau}$$

$$P_t^{quantos} = \left[K N(-d_2) - Z_t e^{(R_f - D')\tau} N(-d_1)\right]\bar{S}e^{-R_d\tau}$$

where

$$d_1 = \frac{\ln\left(\frac{Z_t}{K}\right) + \left(R_f - D' + \frac{\sigma_z^2}{2}\right)}{\sigma_z\sqrt{\tau}}$$

$$d_2 = d_1 - \sigma_z\sqrt{\tau}$$

$$D' = D + \sigma_{ZS}$$

and where D is the continuously compounded dividend yield on the foreign stock index and σ_S and σ_{ZS} are the volatility of the exchange rate and the covariance between the stock market index and the exchange rate, respectively.

The role of the covariance term σ_{ZS} is interesting. To place things in a more familiar context of correlation,

$$\sigma_{ZS} = \rho_{ZS}\sigma_Z\sigma_S$$

where ρ_{zs} is the correlation coefficient between the stock market index and the exchange rate. Quantos calls are inversely related and quantos puts are positively related to the level of correlation between the stock market index and the exchange rate.

Quantos options live in the environment of the over-the-counter market, although listed stock index warrants with quantos features have existed. Usually dealers create quantos options for their institutional asset manager clients on demand. The advantage to the end user is that the quantos delivers currency hedging in precisely the correct face value; in effect, the quantos currency face value rises and falls in precise proportion to the movements in the foreign stock index. On the other side of the transaction stands a dealer who is faced with having to adjust the currency hedge to movements in the foreign stock index. The major problem is that the correlation between the stock market index and the exchange rate might be sufficiently unstable so as to create the risk of significant under- or overhedging. As Piros (1998) points out, the end user should expect to pay for this convenience.

Comments on Hedging with Nonbarrier Currency Options

The world of exotic currency options is a dynamic environment where new options are always being invented. Many new exotic options are nothing more than mathematical whimsy. But occasionally, a useful new exotic currency option is born.

A good rule for knowing when to use exotic options is to look for structures that meet the hedging objectives at a significant cost advantage compared to what would have to be spent for vanilla currency options. This would seem to indicate that there is a free lunch embedded in some varieties of exotic currency options. Rather, the point is that cost savings can materialize when a hedger works to selectively buy what protection she does in fact need without paying for forms of protection that are unwanted.

Average rate currency options are appropriate for the hedger who is interested primarily in the average exchange rate over a period of time. Because average rate options are cheaper than vanilla options, there will be a clear cost savings over buying a vanilla option. In the same way, a basket option saves on hedging expenses provided that the objective is to hedge a portfolio of currencies as opposed to buying protection on one currency at a time.

Compound options can be effective where there is uncertainty about the need to hedge. Rather than commit to the purchase of a vanilla option, the hedger can pay a lower initial premium to buy a compound option and therefore lock in the cost of the hedge in the future if one is needed.

Finally, the quantos option costs money, but it can reduce risk. The defining attribute of a quantos option is that it delivers the correctly sized hedge for a foreign stock index that changes with market conditions.

Bibliography

Abramowitz, Milton, and Irene A. Stegun, eds. *Handbook of Mathematical Functions with Formulas, Graphs, and Mathematical Tables.* Washington, D.C.: National Bureau of Standards, Applied Mathematics Series 55, December 1972.

Association Cambiste Internationale. *Code of Conduct.* Paris: Dremer-Muller & Cie, Foetz, 1991.

Babbel, David F., and Laurence K. Isenberg. "Quantity-Adjusting Options and Forward Contacts." *Journal of Financial Engineering* 2, no. 2 (June 1993): 89–126.

Bachelier, Louis. *Théorie de la Speculation.* Paris: Gauthier-Villars, 1900. Reprinted in *The Random Character of Stock Market Prices,* ed. Paul H. Cootner. Cambridge, Mass.: MIT Press, 1967.

Ball, Clifford A., and Antonio Roma. "Stochastic Volatility Option Pricing." *Journal of Financial and Quantitative Analysis* 29 (December 1994): 589–607.

Bank for International Settlements. "Survey of Foreign Exchange Market Activity." Basle: BIS, 1993 and 1998.

Barone-Adesi, Giovanni, and Robert E. Whaley. "Efficient Analytic Approximation of American Option Values." *Journal of Finance* 42 (June 1987): 301–320. Reprinted in *Currency Derivatives,* ed. David DeRosa. New York: John Wiley & Sons, 1998.

Bates, David S. "Dollar Jump Fears, 1984–1992: Distributional Abnormalities Implicit in Currency Futures Options." *Journal of International Money and Finance* 15, no. 1 (1994): 65–91. Reprinted in *Currency Derivatives,* ed. David DeRosa. New York: John Wiley & Sons, 1998.

———. "Jumps and Stochastic Volatility: Exchange Rate Processes Implicit in Deutsche Mark Options." *Review of Financial Studies* 9, no. 1 (1996): 69–107.

Benson, Robert, and Nicholas Daniel. "Up Over and Out." *Risk* 4 (June 1991): 17–19.

Berger, Eric. "Barrier Options." *Handbook of Exotic Options,* ed. Israel Nelken. Chicago: Irwin Professional Publishing, 1996.

Black, Fischer. "The Pricing of Commodity Contracts." *Journal of Financial Economics* 3 (January–March 1976), 167–179. Reprinted in *Currency Derivatives*, ed. David DeRosa. New York: John Wiley & Sons, 1998.

———. "How We Came Up with the Option Formula." *Journal of Portfolio Management* (Winter 1989): 4–8.

Black, Fischer, and John Cox. "Valuing Corporate Securities: Some Effects of Bond Indenture Provisions." *Journal of Finance* 31 (May 1976): 351–368.

Black, Fischer, and Myron Scholes. "The Pricing of Options and Corporate Liabilities." *Journal of Political Economy* 81 (May–June 1973): 637–659.

Bodurtha, James N, Jr., and Georges R. Courtadon. "Tests of an American Option Pricing Model on the Foreign Currency Options Market." *Journal of Financial and Quantitative Analysis* 22 (June 1987): 153–167.

Bowie, Jonathan and Peter Carr. "Statistic Simplicity." *Risk* 7:8 (August 1994).

Box, G. E. P., and G. M. Jenkins. *Time Series Analysis: Forecasting and Control*. San Francisco: Holden Day, 1970.

Boyle, Phelim P., and David Emanuel. "Mean Dependent Options." Working paper, University of Waterloo, Ontario, Canada, 1985.

Boyle, Phelim P., and S. H. Lau. "Bumping Up against the Barrier with the Binomial Method." *Journal of Derivatives* 1,4 (1994): 6–14.

Brennan, M. J., Georges Courtadon, and Marti Subrahmanyam. "Options on the Spot and Options on Futures." *Journal of Finance* 40 (December 1985): 1303–1317.

Brennan, M. J., and E. S. Schwartz. "The Valuation of American Put Options." *Journal of Finance* 32 (May 1977): 449–462.

Brenner, Menachem, and Marti G. Subrahmanyam. "A Simple Approach to Option Valuation and Hedging in the Black-Scholes Model." *Financial Analyst Journal* (March/April 1994): 25–28.

Briys, Eric, M. Bellalah, H. M. Mai, and F. de Varenne. *Options, Futures, and Exotic Derivatives*. Chichester: John Wiley & Sons, 1998.

Bunch, David S., and Herb Johnson. "The American Put Option and Its Critical Stock Price." Forthcoming. *Journal of Finance.*

Campa, Jose Manuel, and P. H. Kevin Chang. "Learning From the Term Structure of Implied Volatility in Foreign Exchange Options." *Cur-*

rency Options and Exchange Rate Economics, ed. Zhaohui Chen. Singapore: World Scientific Publishing, 1998.

Carr, Peter. "European Put Call Symmetry." Working paper, Cornell University, Ithaca, New York, 1994.

Carr, Peter, Katrina Ellis, and Vishal Gupta. "Static Hedging of Exotic Options." *Journal of Finance* 53, no. 3 (June 1998): 1165–1190.

Chang, Carolyn W., and Jack K. Chang. "Forward and Futures Prices: Evidence from the Foreign Exchange Markets." *The Journal of Finance* 45 (September 1990): 1333–1336.

Chesney, M., and L. Scott. "Pricing European Currency Options: A Comparison of the Modified Black-Scholes Model and a Random Variance Model." *Journal of Financial and Quantitative Analysis* 24 (September 1989): 267–284. Reprinted in *Currency Derivatives*, ed. David DeRosa. New York: John Wiley & Sons, 1998.

Chriss, Neil A. *Black-Scholes and Beyond*. Chicago: Irwin Professional Publishing, 1997.

Cornell, Bradford, and Marc R. Reinganum. "Forward and Futures Prices: Evidence from the Foreign Exchange Markets." *Journal of Finance* 36, no. 12 (December 1981): 1035–1045. Reprinted in *Currency Derivatives*, ed. David DeRosa. New York: John Wiley & Sons, 1998.

Cox, John C., Jonathon E. Ingersoll, and Stephen A. Ross. "The Relationship Between Forward and Futures Prices." *Journal of Financial Economics* 9 (December 1981): 321–346. Reprinted in *Currency Derivatives*, ed. David DeRosa. New York: John Wiley & Sons, 1998.

Cox, John C., and Stephen A. Ross. "The Valuation of Options for Alternative Stochastic Processes." *Journal of Financial Economics* 3 (January–March 1976): 145–166.

Cox, John C., Stephen A. Ross, and Mark Rubinstein. "Option Pricing: A Simplified Approach." *Journal of Financial Economics* 7 (September 1979): 229–263.

Cox, John C., and Mark Rubinstein. *Options Markets*. Englewood Cliffs, N.J.: Prentice-Hall, 1985.

Derman, Emanuel. "Reflections on Fisher." *Journal of Portfolio Management* (December 1996):18–24.

———. "Regimes of Volatility" (internal research publication). New York: Goldman, Sachs & Co., January 1999.

———. "Riding on a Smile." *Risk* 7 (February 1994a): 32–39.

Derman, Emanuel, and Iraj Kani. "The Volatility Smile and Its Implied Tree." New York: Goldman, Sachs & Co., January 1994b.

Derman, Emanuel, Iraj Kani, and Neil Chriss. "Implied Trinomial Trees of the Volatility Smile" (internal research publication). New York: Goldman, Sachs & Co., February 1996.

Derman, Emanuel, Iraj Kani, and Joseph Z. Zou. "The Local Volatility Surface" (internal research publication). New York: Goldman, Sachs & Co., December 1995.

Derman, Emanuel, Piotr Karasinski, and Jeffrey S. Wecker. "Understanding Guaranteed Exchange-Rate Contracts in Foreign Stock Investments" (internal research publication). New York: Goldman, Sachs & Co., 1990.

DeRosa, David F. *Managing Foreign Exchange Risk.* Rev. ed. Chicago: Irwin Professional Publishing, 1996.

———. *Currency Derivatives.* New York: John Wiley & Sons, 1998.

Dravid, Ajay, Mathew Richardson, and Tong-sheng Sun. "Pricing Foreign Index Contingent Claims: An Application to Nikkei Index Warrants." *Journal of Derivatives* 1 (1993): 33–51. Reprinted in *Currency Derivatives,* ed. David DeRosa. New York: John Wiley & Sons, 1998.

———. "The Pricing of Dollar-Denominated Yen/DM Warrants." *Journal of International Money and Finance* 13, no. 5 (1994): 517–536.

Dupire, Bruno. "Arbitrage Pricing with Stochastic Volatility." In *Proceedings of the AFFI Conference of June 1992.*

———. "Pricing with a Smile." *Risk* 7 no. 1 (January 1994): 18–20.

Fama, Eugene F. "Forward and Spot Exchange Rates." *Journal of Monetary Economics* 14 (1984): 319–338.

Freidman, Daniel, and Stoddard Vandersteel. "Short-Run Fluctuations in Foreign Exchange Rates: Evidence from the Data 1973–79." *Journal of International Economics* 13 (1982): 171–186.

Froot, Kenneth A. "Currency Hedging over Long Horizons." Working paper no. 4355, National Bureau of Economic Research, New York, May 1993.

Froot, Kenneth A., and Jeffrey A. Frankel. "Forward Discount Bias: Is It an Exchange Risk Premium?" *Quarterly Journal of Economics* 104 (February 1989): 139–161.

Froot, Kenneth A., and Richard A. Thaler. "Anomalies—Foreign Exchange." *Journal of Economic Perspectives* 4, no. 3 (Summer 1990): 179–192.

Funabashi, Yoichi. *Managing the Dollar: From the Plaza to the Louvre.* 2d ed. Washington, D.C.: Institute for International Economics, 1989.

Garman, Mark B., and Michael J. Klass. "On the Estimation of Security Price Volatilities from Historical Data." *Journal of Business* 53 (January 1980): 67–78.

Garman, Mark B., and Steven V. Kohlhagen. "Foreign Currency Option Values." *Journal of International Money and Finance* 2 (December 1983): 231–237. Reprinted in *Currency Derivatives,* ed. David DeRosa. New York: John Wiley & Sons, 1998.

Geman, Helyette, and Marc Yor. "Pricing and Hedging Double-Barrier Options: A Probabilistic Approach." *Mathematical Finance* 6, no. 4 (1996): 365–378. Reprinted in *Currency Derivatives,* ed. David DeRosa. New York: John Wiley & Sons, 1998.

Gemmill, Gordon. *Options Pricing.* Berkshire, England: McGraw-Hill, 1993.

Geske, Robert. "The Valuation of Compound Options." *Journal of Financial Economics* 7 (March 1979): 63–81.

Geske, Robert, and H. E. Johnson. "The American Put Option Valued Analytically." *Journal of Finance* 39 (December 1984): 1511–1524.

Giavazzi, Francesco, and Alberto Giovanninni. *Limiting Exchange Rate Flexibility: The European Monetary System.* Cambridge, Mass.: MIT Press, 1989.

Gibson, Rajna. *Option Valuation.* New York: McGraw-Hill, 1991.

Grabbe, J. Orlin. "The Pricing of Call and Put Options on Foreign Exchange." *Journal of International Money and Finance* 2 (1983):239–253.

———. *International Financial Markets.* Englewood Cliffs, N.J.: Prentice-Hall, 1996.

Haug, Espen Gaarder. *The Complete Guide to Option Pricing Formulas.* New York: McGraw-Hill, 1998.

Heston, Steven L. "A Closed Form Solution for Options with Stochastic Volatility with Applications to Bond and Currency Options." *Review of Financial Studies* 6, no. 2 (1993): 327–343.

Ho, T. S., Richard C. Stapleton, and Marti G. Subrahmanyam. "A Simple Technique for the Valuation and Hedging of American Options." *Journal of Derivatives* (Fall 1994): 52–66.

Hsieh, David. "Testing for Nonlinear Dependence in Daily Foreign Exchange Rates." *Journal of Business* 62 (1989): 339–368.

Hsu, Hans. "Practical Pointers on Basket Options." *International Treasurer,* May 15, 1995, 4–7.

———. "Surprised Parties." *Risk* 10, no. 4 (April 1997): 27–29.

Hudson, Mike. "The Value of Going Out." Risk 4, no. 3 (March 1991): 29–33.

Hui, Cho H. "One-Touch Double Barrier Binary Option Values." *Applied Financial Economics* no. 6 (1996): 343–346. Reprinted in *Currency Derivatives,* ed. David DeRosa. New York: John Wiley & Sons, 1998.

Hull, John C. *Options, Futures and Other Derivatives.* 3d ed. Englewood Cliffs, NJ: Prentice-Hall, 1997.

Hull, John, and Alan White. "The Pricing of Options on Assets with Stochastic Volatilities." *Journal of Finance* 42 (June 1987): 281–300.

International Monetary Fund. *Exchange Arrangements and Exchange Restrictions.* Washington, D.C.: International Monetary Fund, 1994.

International Swaps and Derivatives Association. *1998 FX and Currency Option Definitions.* New York: International Swaps and Derivatives Association, 1998.

Jarrow, Robert A., and Andrew Rudd. *Option Pricing.* Homewood, Ill.: Dow Jones-Irwin, 1983.

Jorion, Philippe. "On Jump Processes in the Foreign Exchange and Stock Markets." *Review of Financial Studies* 1, no. 4 (1989): 427–445. Reprinted in *Currency Derivatives,* ed. David DeRosa. New York: John Wiley & Sons, 1998.

Jorion, Philippe, and Neal M. Stoughton. "An Empirical Investigation of the Early Exercise Premium of Foreign Currency Options." *Journal of Futures Markets* 9 (1989a): 365–375.

———. "Test of the Early Exercise Premium Using the Foreign Currency Options Market." In *Recent Developments in International Banking and Finance,* ed. S. Khoury. Chicago: Probus, 1989b.

Kemna, A. G. Z., and C. F. Vorst. "A Pricing Method for Options Based on Average Asset Values." *Journal of Banking and Finance* 14 (1990): 113–129.

Kendall, M., and A. Stuart. *The Advanced Theory of Statistics*. Vol. 1. London: Charles Griffin, 1943.

Keynes, John Maynard. *A Tract on Monetary Reform*. London: Macmillan, 1923.

Kim, In Joon. "The Analytic Valuation of American Options." *Review of Financial Studies* 3 (1990): 547–572.

Kunitomo, N., and M. Ikeda. "Pricing Options with Curved Barriers." *Mathematical Finance* 2, no. 4 (1992): 275–298.

Levy, Edmond. "Asian Arithmetic." *Risk* 3 (May 1990): 7–8.

———. "Pricing of European Average Rate Currency Options." *Journal of International Money and Finance* 11 (1992): 474–491. Reprinted in *Currency Derivatives*, ed. David DeRosa. New York: John Wiley & Sons, 1998.

Levy, P. *Processus Stochastiques et Mouvement Brownien*. Paris: Gauthier-Villars, 1948.

Liu, Christina, and Jia He. "A Variance-Ratio Test of Random Walks in Foreign Exchange Rates." *Journal of Finance* 46, no. 2 (June 1991): 773–785.

MacMillan, Lionel W. "Approximation for the American Put Option." *Advances in Futures and Options Research*. Vol 1. Greenwich, Conn.: JAI Press, 1986.

Malz, Allan M. "Using Option Prices to Estimate Realignment Probabilities in the European Monetary System: The Case of Sterling-Mark." *Journal of International Money and Finance* 15, no. 5 (1996): 717–748.

———. "Estimating the Probability Distribution of the Future Exchange Rate from Option Prices." *Journal of Derivatives* (Winter 1997): 18–36.

———. "An Introduction to Currency Option Markets." In *Currency Options and Exchange Rate Economics*, ed. Zhaohui Chen. Singapore: World Scientific Publishing, 1998.

Margrabe, William. "A Theory of Forward and Futures Prices." Working paper, Wharton School, University of Pennsylvania, Philadelphia, 1976.

————. "The Value of an Option to Exchange One Asset for Another." *Journal of Finance* 33 (March 1978): 177–186.

————. "Average Options." Working paper, Bankers Trust Company, New York, 1990.

McFarland, James W., R. Richardson Pettit, and Sam K. Sung. "The Distribution of Foreign Exchange Price Changes: Trading Day Effects and Risk Measurement." *Journal of Finance* 37, no. 3 (June 1982): 693–715.

Merton, Robert C. "Theory of Rational Option Pricing." *Bell Journal of Economics and Management Science* 4 (Spring 1973): 141–183.

————. "Option Pricing when Underlying Stock Returns Are Discontinuous." *Journal of Financial Economics* 3 (January/March 1976): 99–118.

Parkinson, Michael. "Option Pricing: The American Put." *Journal of Business* 50 (January 1977): 21–36.

————. "The Extreme Value Method for Estimating the Variance of the Rate of Return." *Journal of Business* 53 (January 1980): 61–65.

Perold, Andre F., and Evan C. Schulman. "The Free Lunch in Currency Hedging: Implications for Investment Policy and Performance Standard." *Financial Analysts Journal* (May/June 1988): 45–50.

Piros, Christopher D. "The Perfect Hedge: To Quanto or Not to Quanto." In *Currency Derivatives*, ed. David DeRosa. New York: John Wiley & Sons, 1998.

Press, William H., Brian P. Flannery, Saul A. Teukolsky, and William T. Vetterling. *Numerical Recipes*. Cambridge, Mass.: Cambridge University Press, 1986.

Reiner, Eric. "Quanto Mechanics." *Risk* 5 (March 1992): 59–63.

Reiner, Eric, and Mark Rubinstein. "Breaking Down the Barriers." *Risk* 4 (September 1991a): 29–35.

————. "Unscrambling the Binary Code." *Risk* 4 (October 1991b): 75–83.

Rich, Don. "The Mathematical Foundations of Barrier Option-Pricing Theory." In *Advances in Futures Options Research*. Vol. 7, ed. Don M. Chance and Robert R. Trippi. Greenwich, Conn.: JAI Press, 1994.

Ritchken, Peter. "On Pricing Barrier Options." *Journal of Derivatives* 3 (1995): 19–28. Reprinted in *Currency Derivatives*, ed. David DeRosa. New York: John Wiley & Sons, 1998.

Rubinstein, Mark. "Exotic Options." Unpublished manuscript, University of California–Berkeley, 1990.

———. "Options for the Undecided." *Risk* 4 (April 1991): 43.

———. "Implied Binomial Trees." *Journal of Finance* 69, no. 3 (July 1994): 771–818.

Ruttiens, Alain. "Classical Replica." *Risk* 3 (February 1990): 33–36.

Schwartz, Eduardo S. "The Valuation of Warrants: Implementing a New Approach." *Journal of Financial Economics* 4 (1977): 79–93.

Scott, L. "Option Pricing when the Variance Changes Randomly: Theory, Estimation, and an Application." *Journal of Financial and Quantitative Analysis* 22 (December 1987): 419–438.

Stein, E. M., and C. J. Stein. "Stock Price Distributions with Stochastic Volatility: An Analytic Approach." *Review of Financial Studies* 4 (1991): 727–752.

Stoll, Hans R., and Robert E. Whaley. "New Options Instruments: Arbitrage-able Linkages and Valuation." *Advances in Futures and Options Research.* Vol. 1. Greenwich, Conn.: JAI Press, 1986.

Taleb, Nassim. *Dynamic Hedging.* New York: John Wiley & Sons, 1997.

Taylor, Stephen J., and Xinzhong Xu. "The Magnitude of Implied Volatility: Smiles Theory and Empirical Evidence for Exchange Rates." *Review of Futures Markets* 13 (1994): 355–380. Reprinted in *Currency Derivatives*, ed. David DeRosa. New York: John Wiley & Sons, 1998.

Turnbull, S. M., and L. M. Wakeman. "A Quick Algorithm for Pricing European Average Options." *Journal of Financial and Quantitative Analysis* 26 (1991): 377–389.

Wasserfallen, Walter. "Flexible Exchange Rates: A Closer Look." *Journal of Monetary Economics* 23 (1989): 511–521.

Wasserfallen, Walter, and Heinz Zimmermann. "The Behavior of Intra-Daily Exchange Rates." *Journal of Banking and Finance* 9 (1985): 55–72.

Westerfield, Janice M. "Empirical Properties of Foreign Exchange Rates under Fixed and Floating Rate Regimes." *Journal of International Economics* 7 (June 1977): 181–200.

Whaley, Robert E. "On Valuing American Futures Options." *Financial Analysts Journal* 42 (May/June 1986): 194–204. Reprinted in *Currency Derivatives*, ed. David DeRosa. New York: John Wiley & Sons, 1998.

Wiggins, J. B. "Option Values under Stochastic Volatility: Theory and Empirical Estimates." *Journal of Financial Economics* 19 (1987): 351–372.

Xu, Xinzhong, and Stephen J. Taylor. "The Term Structure of Volatility Implied by Foreign Exchange Options." *Journal of Financial and Quantitative Analysis* 29, no. 1 (March 1994): 57–73. Reprinted in *Currency Derivatives*, ed. David DeRosa. New York: John Wiley & Sons, 1998.

Index